Links of
Forever

Links of Forever

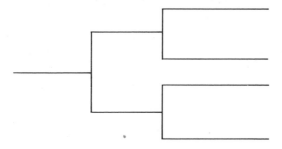

INSPIRATIONAL STORIES OF LINEAGE AND LOVE

Compiled by Connie Rector
and Diane Deputy

BOOKCRAFT, INC.
Salt Lake City, Utah

Library of Congress Catalog Card Number: 77-74766
ISBN 0-88494-315-1

First Printing, 1977

Lithographed in the United States of America
PUBLISHERS PRESS
Salt Lake City, Utah

Preface

Every member of The Church of Jesus Christ of Latter-day Saints has a responsibility from the Lord to work for his kindred dead — establishing clear genealogical links and providing the vicarious saving ordinances in the temple. The deep sense of joy accruing from this work transforms that duty into pleasure.

Why the requirement and why the joy? The scriptures and the "spirit of Elijah" give us the answer.

The prophet Malachi foretold Elijah's latter-day appearance (Malachi 4:5-6), and in 1823 the angel Moroni sharpened the focus when he gave the youthful Joseph Smith this rendering of Malachi's words:

"Behold, I will reveal unto you the Priesthood, by the hand of Elijah the prophet, before the coming of the great and dreadful day of the Lord.

"And he shall plant in the hearts of the children the promises made to the fathers, and the hearts of the children shall turn to their fathers.

"If it were not so, the whole earth would be utterly wasted at his coming." (D&C 2:1-3.)

This prophecy was fulfilled on April 3, 1836, when the resurrected Elijah appeared to the Prophet Joseph Smith in the Kirtland Temple and restored to the earth the fulness of the power of the priesthood. This priesthood, as held by Elijah during his earthly ministry, confers on mortal prophets, duly commissioned by the Lord, the keys of binding and sealing on earth and in heaven all the ordinances and principles pertaining to the salvation of mankind.

v

Through the spirit and influence of Elijah, "the hearts of the children shall turn to their fathers" in love and concern. That is the reason why ever since Elijah's visit there has been an increasing interest in genealogy: genealogical societies formed, individuals and families gathering genealogical records, both Latter-day Saints and others pursuing with ever-heightening fascination the research which establishes their lineage.

Most important, while many organizations and individuals are gathering and compiling ancestral data, The Church of Jesus Christ of Latter-day Saints is unique in *doing* something with this information. It is linking names together into proven families and then providing the saving, sealing ordinances for those families at an ever-increasing pace as the Church expands and temples multiply. It is welding families into an eternal union in the patriarchal order.

Furthering the mission of Elijah, many Church members are doing their part to ensure that the earth shall not be wasted at the Savior's coming. They are preparing their own book of remembrance — a book for presentation "in his holy temple, . . . a book containing the records of our dead, which shall be worthy of all acceptation." (D&C 128:24.)

But many more Latter-day Saints need to be involved in this crucial work for themselves and their departed ancestors. ". . . It is important," said the Prophet Joseph Smith; "and . . . this is the spirit of Elijah, that we redeem our dead, and connect ourselves with our fathers which are in heaven, and seal up our dead to come forth in the first resurrection. . . ." Without our departed ancestors, he told us, we cannot be made perfect. (*Documentary History of the Church*, volume 6, page 252.)

Links of Forever is not a genealogical textbook. Rather it is a collection of first-hand twentieth-century accounts telling of exciting and successful experiences in genealogical research. The stories depict varied problems and different ways in which help came to solve them.

Everyone who desires to can perform this labor of love. Nor does he need to be alone in his search. There are no barriers to the Lord. As this book shows, help has come to others. It can come also to you. If you will get started and then keep going, you too can know the joy and excitement of involvement in this great latter-day work.

CONNIE DANIEL RECTOR
DIANE DREIER DEPUTY

Contents

IV Journeys to Ancestral Areas

V Valuable Records Preserved

VI Directed by Dreams

VII Help from Those Beyond

I

Led to Records

Question:

If we work hard and long enough, will we eventually find the records we need? Haven't there been times when people have been directed "spiritually" to certain records?

"There Is Something in There for You"

Ivy Larsen

It was a great inconvenience, but the rule had been changed. Now the employees who helped us get our films for the reading machines could all go to lunch at the same time. Previously their lunch times had been staggered so that someone was always there to get out films for us. Slips for films we wanted to use must now be filled out as early as twenty or thirty minutes before lunch time in order to have the film back and on the reader for use. It was a big rush, the last few minutes. If a person did not get the film he wanted, he had to wait until the employees returned from lunch.

How I wished, along with many other researchers, that I could go back and get my own film and thread it on the reader myself! I knew how to do it, but the rule was that the employees were to do it for the researchers. I looked at the clock and knew I had to hurry and get my film ordered in order to keep on working. I hurriedly took off the film I had on the reader, filled out the slip for another parish register film, and turned it in. Now I had to sit back and wait or study my sheets to make my plans for the search I was making for a patron. Time seemed to drag while I waited, and I felt the urgent need to hurry. Research time was rare and valuable.

Finally the film came, it was put on the reader and the

3

employees left for lunch. I turned to the first page, a table of contents for the film. To my absolute dismay it was a probate record, not the parish record I had wanted. Either I had written down the wrong call number in my haste or the girl had picked up the wrong film in her hurry to go to lunch. I was deeply disappointed; and, thinking about the many minutes that I was to lose, I very abruptly put my hand on the handle to whirl it off. But my hand was stopped.

"Don't take it off! There is something in there for you." A voice had spoken to me.

Surprised, I answered, "If there is something in there for me, just what am I looking for?"

I hadn't the slightest idea what I wanted in that film. I had used the probates before and I knew they gave very valuable information. But for whom was I looking?

I felt instructed, "Go to the index in the back of the film and see if something rings a bell."

I turned to the index and checked every name. Four names interested me to some extent, but there was nothing definite. I wrote down the names and page numbers and followed through, one at a time, looking up their probates until I had checked three of them. Nothing! These were not mine!

"Then this must be just my imagination," I said to myself. I was rather annoyed, and feeling that I was wasting my time I put my hand on the handle again to whirl it off. Again my hand was stopped!

"Look up the fourth one."

Dutifully I looked up the last name I had copied. To my amazement it was the probate of the sister of the ancestor whose sheet I had put aside. I had not been able to find anymore for the ancestor and her husband. In fact, I had put the sheet aside several times and as many times had picked it up again, feeling

4

that there must be something more. I was at the beginning of the parish register with her and I could not reach beyond that time; at least, I had come to that conclusion. I had searched the probate records for her but she was not listed in the index. I had her sheet in my case. I opened the case, laid the family group sheet before me, and turned back to the film.

What a probate! Dorthe Christoffersen had named her parents, her brothers and sisters, and her sisters' husbands and where they resided. She named her sister Maren (my ancestor) and her husband, which I had on my sheet; also their children, which I also had. This proved this was the right family in the probate. She named a deceased brother and his children and others, totaling five families in all. I could not believe it! I just sat there and stared at it!

As soon as I composed myself, I wrote the information down on family group sheets. This took the pedigree line one generation back before the parish register started, and by naming the children and their places of residence it brought them back into the parish registers. This was a "gold mine."

I went back to the index and found the page number for the probate of the deceased brother. Here again, the same families were named and the children given, along with the name of the brother's wife. In the excitement the "find" had stimulated, I was oblivious to the time and to anything and anybody around me.

Over the next several days I brought the descendants of these families down through the parish registers into the period of time for census records and military levying rolls, etc. When I had the family group sheets completed and ready to turn in for clearance, there were the names of over four hundred people to be submitted for temple work to be done. A whole congregation of people! And all because a "wrong" film was put on the machine!

Something,
However Small

L. Ferrin Lindsey

For years I had been intending to start working on my genealogy, but something would always seem to be more important at the time (another new baby, opening my own business, a new Church calling, etc.). Still, the feeling would come now and then that I should do *something*, however small. After taking several ward genealogy courses I realized that this alone was not getting my ancestors identified and their temple work completed. My wife and I finally determined to set aside two hours a week on Wednesday nights, while our older children were at MIA and our younger ones were in bed. (We have eleven children, so our time was very limited.)

For four months we faithfully spent two hours every week writing letters, gathering all available information from the known family genealogists. We compiled our Book of Remembrance and did many other genealogy-related things, including handing in our four-generation sheets.

One cold February morning, just after two big snowstorms, the snow was piled higher than the cars on both sides of the streets. I had to go to my office to help some of the salesmen. As I pulled up to a stoplight on the way to work, a voice said, "Turn right, and go down to the Genealogical Library." (I normally turn left at that particular light.) Without even thinking I turned right and drove toward the library. I thought: "What am I doing? I've got to be at the office right away. I have no reason in the world to be going to the Genealogical Library!"

But a tremendous desire came upon me to continue toward the library. When I arrived, the only parking was in the middle of the street because of the piles of snow in the parking areas. I said to myself, "This is crazy. I can't even park. I'll just go on to the office." But again this voice within me told me to go to the Library *now*. Finally I parked the car on a side street and entered the library.

This was the first time I had ever been to the Genealogical Library, so I had no idea what to do. I went to a desk and asked for assistance. When the worker there asked where my ancestors had lived, I remembered a location on one of the family group sheets we had been working on the previous Wednesday evening — Owen County, Indiana. He directed me to a card file; and as we began going through the cards, at his suggestion I wrote down film numbers and other information for possible records to search.

After going through twenty or thirty of these cards we came to one that made my heart leap within me. I took the film number down and asked where I could get the film and a film reader. The library worker wanted to continue through the file, checking for more possible sources, but my mind would not leave that particular film. I had a great desire to get it and find out what it contained.

I located the film and someone helped me put it on. I had no idea what I was looking for, so I just kept turning until I came to a place with several hundred marriage entries. In the center of all those names, two almost leaped out at me. I was so surprised that I was shaking with excitement. These two names were the marriage entry for my third great-grandfather and great-grandmother.

7

When my wife and I went to the temple to do the marriage sealing for this couple, a very beautiful feeling came over us and tears of joy streamed down our faces.

I have since been back to that film and copied the names of many other ancestors and had their temple work done. We have also found many other ancestors and had the work done for them. That original experience is just one of the many I have received in doing this work.

I know with all my heart that genealogical and temple work is one of the most beautiful parts of the gospel of Jesus Christ. I look forward with great excitement to the time when I can meet some of my ancestors and rejoice with them at the help and direction of our Heavenly Father in these matters. I have a testimony that we can in a special way follow our Savior, by placing within our ancestors' grasp the salvation he offers to us all.

They Wanted to Be Found

Rose Hinton

While working at a film machine one day in the Genealogical Library, I noted an Ellis name. It was not an Ellis from my family, but it reminded me of my ancestor Ephraim Ellis, who was the earliest I had found on his line. The thought came to me to go up to the archives and look for his family group sheet.

I argued in my mind that I had already done that, and I knew the sheet was not there. The impression continued, however, so I went up to check again.

It turned out that there was a sheet for an Ephraim Ellis, but he was not mine. This one was for an earlier date and was from Massachusetts; mine had been in Vermont. I looked alphabetically for this Ephraim's father, Malachi Ellis, but the sheet was not where it should have been in the book.

I decided to have this Ephraim's sheet copied anyway, and I rose to take the book up to the copy machine. As I picked up the binder it opened in my hand, and there lay the sheet of Malachi Ellis. It had been misfiled.

I knew then that I needed to have both sheets copied, and I looked to see who Malachi's father was. It was Matthias Ellis, but his sheet was not in the binder either.

At the xerox counter I pointed out to the attendant the one sheet that had been misfiled and said that while she was copying the two sheets I would find the correct place where the misfiled page should go.

As I took hold of the book it opened in my hand again; and there lay the sheet of Matthias Ellis, which had also been misfiled!

I realized then that these *must* be *my people*, so after the copying was done I went to the source of information given on the Matthias family group sheet. In a very few minutes I had learned that Matthias Ellis was the great-grandfather of my Ephraim Ellis, and that his temple work, and that of those intervening generations I had found that day, had all been done.

What is more, I spent the next three hours in the archives tracing the Ellis and related lines.

I realized then more strongly even than before that it is not only important to find new information with which to have temple work done; it is also important to have a copy of what has already been completed. Subsequently, and perhaps most significantly, I was able to make additions and corrections to some of the sheets.

Mourning Pool

William A. Pope, Jr.

Our Farmington, New Mexico, stake genealogical seminar was an outstanding success! The chapel was filled to the brim with enthusiastic, genealogy-minded Saints, including over a hundred youth. The spirit there was indeed powerful and bore testimony to us often of the importance of genealogical and temple work.

The reports handed to me as president of the stake caused me to experience not only deep feelings of joy but humility as well as I felt the promptings of the Spirit to begin my own research. But why?

My grandfather had been faithful in accomplishing much vicarious work for our ancestors in his lifetime. How could I improve on his diligent efforts? I decided to find out for myself. Since time was an important factor, I engaged a family researcher whom we as a family further supported with our faith and prayers.

Though I had only a few family records in my possession, I felt sure there would be literally hundreds of records on file in the Salt Lake City Genealogical Library. Unfortunately, an archive search there did not confirm this. I was astounded! What had happened to Grandfather's records? A short time later I received from the researcher a book of remembrance containing a small group of archive sheets on my family lines. I was disappointed to

11

find that there were only a few more family sheets than I had given her in the beginning. They were in order, however, and since some progress was being made on the research, I experienced some feeling of satisfaction, however small.

Over a period of time several more letters arrived from the researcher indicating some unusual experiences she had had in connection with the archive records. She wrote:

"The Spirit of the Lord was very strong the day I searched the archives for your family group sheets. Hoping to extend your pedigree, I located the sheet of Jonathon Pool, born March 23, 1796, and his wife and ten children. His father was listed simply William Pool. The mother's name was not recorded. A further check for a William Pool of the age to be Jonathon's father was not found.

"Returning to the table to continue my work of compilation of the sheets I had just gathered, I received a strong impression to *again* search the Pool records. Puzzled, I returned and searched for Jonathon's father (under some other name perhaps?) but was not successful. "Strange," I thought, and a second time I went back to my work. This time, however, the Spirit was so strong that I was literally drawn from my chair and pulled back (or so it seemed) to the binders containing the Pool names. Although I had prayed before, I knew that I must deepen my prayers in order to merit the inspiration necessary to find this Pool record — whatever it was.

"A third check revealed nothing. Still praying, I noticed again a William Pool, born 1744 in North Carolina, *not* Virginia, and wife Mary, who was much too early to be our William, the father of Jonathon. I had skimmed over it before — but wait! This William Pool, born 1744, did have a son William who could have been the one we were looking for. Only his name and approximate date of birth were listed. Suddenly a notation at the bottom of the sheet "stood out." 'William Pool Sr. and family moved from North Carolina to Virginia about 1793, from Muddy Creek to Elk

Creek, Grayson County, Virginia.' Our Jonathon Pool, Sr. had been born in 1796 in Elk Creek, Virginia. The William Pool, Sr. and wife Mary were the grandparents of our Jonathon Pool! I knew by the Spirit that this was true. Further research confirmed this as fact.

"Jonathon Pool's father William did leave a will in 1836, but named only his three daughters, Piety, Rebecca, and *Mourning*. In a later land record of 1847, Jonathon Pool states that he is the son of William, deceased, while an earlier land entry had listed Jonathon as a brother to Rebecca, Piety, and Mourning Pool. A land grant from the state of Virginia to William Sr. proved conclusively his time and place of entry into Grayson County. Earlier North Carolina records also confirm his residence there and an early grant to an Edward Pool pinpoint him as a possible ancestor of William Sr.!"

With this and other evidence, special permission was granted for the temple work to be done, sealing Jonathon and his sisters to their father William of the archive sheet who was already sealed to his father, William Sr. and his mother, Mary. Three generations of Pools!

Some months later, Grandfather's records were found, copied, and sent to the researcher. She was amazed at the extensiveness and seeming accuracy of Grandfather's work. The sheets were all neatly typed and in perfect order. She must have wondered if her own work might have been in vain. For there, in the family records, were completed sheets on Jonathon Pool, his father William Pool, and the grandparents William Sr. and Mary Pool. Sources listed were knowledge of relatives through personal visits to Virginia as well as other varied records Grandfather had searched.

Why had the researcher been directed by the Spirit to do research on the ancestors of Jonathon Pool? The answer came through direction of the Spirit and a reexamination of Grand-

13

father's records. Despite Grandfather's diligent and careful work, *Mourning Pool*, the daughter of William, had been overlooked! Additional research had proven her existence.

Could there possibly be a "Mourning Pool" (or someone like her) missing from other sheets also? A further check of the Pool records indicated this to be the case. By further research we managed to correct these omissions.

Grandfather did the very best he could with what records were available in his generation. Surely his work had been worthy of acceptance. Now, though, in our generation, are we not responsible to do the best that we can with the *further* knowledge available to us?

I have had great love and admiration for my grandfather. He has contributed much to my testimony of the truthfulness of the gospel of Jesus Christ and to genealogical and temple work. I am striving to live up to his example by rechecking and proving his records, that they may be complete and worthy of acceptation before the Lord.

I Found Success

Lucy Price

The Jordan wind blew icy cold that morning and gray clouds of doubt seemed to filter down from leaden skies to penetrate my heart and make me feel that something was wrong. An occasional chest pain seemed to confirm this as fact. Perhaps I should no longer try to pursue my family genealogy. Others could do it better, I thought, by finding records and experiencing spiritual happenings, but not me. Oh, it seemed all so useless — and so many other things needed my attention, too!

All too soon, my friend came to pick me up. I had not even the heart to tell her I wouldn't go. (Genealogical research meant so much to her.) But somehow, sensing my discouragement and lassitude, she inquired about my health. Though I tried my best to be cheerful, I soon found myself sharing my feelings with her. Since we had both been "under the weather" for a long time, we decided to place our names on the temple prayer list; and we did so immediately by telephone. Then, after a combined prayer for strength and health, faith and inspiration, as well as for increased abilities and opportunities, we set out for the Genealogical Library.

My friend and I sat down at one of the reference tables, made plans for the day, and parted after agreeing to meet later, before going home. With less hope than determination I approached again the early Tennessee land and tax records, rather dreading the microfilm machine.

A few minutes later my friend came hurrying over with an excited, happy expression, wildly gesticulating and not making any sense in what she said. Drawing me back to one of the reference tables, she triumphantly pointed to a large volume of some kind of history. Utah! *Pioneers and Prominent Men.* Looking closer, I saw that the book contained pictures and a story of an ancestor I had been seeking! (It seemed she had practically grabbed the book out of the hands of a young man, with only a small "please" and "thank you," since she had felt so strongly impressed to obtain the book immediately.) What a thrill! We made copies for my own records and then each returned to our original tasks.

Some weary hours later, having obtained some not-too-impressive dates and leads to follow, I returned again to our original table. My friend was already there, deeply engrossed in her "large green volume." (Probably another of her inspired "finds," I thought.) I felt tired and a little discouraged again.

She looked up, smiled, and then commended me for finding such a *valuable book*. I must have had a blank look on my face. What was she talking about?

"What book?" I asked, looking about for something familiar. "I didn't find any book." And then as an afterthought, "Isn't that your book?"

She disclaimed any knowledge of it and must have by then been reflecting my expression. "Are you sure?" she asked, un-believing. I nodded in assent. "Yes, are you?" Another nod.

"But, just look here!" she cried. "Why, I just came down a few minutes early and found this old, dark green volume, *Genealogical Surveys, L.D.S. Members,* lying on the table. I decided to leaf through it while waiting for you. It just seemed to 'fall open' to your family record!"

16

I was amazed at the valuable information the record contained! Written by the hand of my pioneer ancestor, Wilson Gardner Perkins, who had crossed the plains as a pioneer, it described the joys and trials of their journey and concluded with his solemn testimony of the truthfulness of the gospel. What a treasure! Then I noticed on the next page a genealogical record which extended several generations back to my immigrant ancestor. And all by personal knowledge of my great-grandfather who lived in the early 1800s. I was overwhelmed.

As my friend and I stared at one another in disbelief, a certain realization seemed to hit us both at the same time.

"How did this book get here?" our thoughts seemed to echo, and at that moment the Spirit of the Lord bore witness to the fact that this book had been *placed* there for us to find.

We were very excited and happy, and extremely grateful to the Lord for this valuable family record which would inspire and direct the way for further research on my pioneer lines.

Truly the Lord had answered my prayers that day and blessed me with a beautiful testimony of the truthfulness of the work I was engaged in.

I *could* succeed in genealogy, I realized! I could find records and experience spiritual happenings as well as others. If I continued with faith and perseverance, the Lord would always open the way.

Bromberg

Diane Dreier Deputy

The first time I saw it the name *Bromberg* was inscribed on a large tombstone in a Jewish cemetery near San Francisco, California. There was a Hebrew inscription as well as the name and death date of my husband's great-grandmother:

> Pauline Harris — native of Bromberg, Prussia died 20 Apr. 1895 — age 72 years (Our Mother)

The next time was several years later in the Genealogical Library in Salt Lake City. With a group of women I had traveled there from Whittier, California. This particular trip I was busily engaged on my own lines when I overheard the name *Bromberg* as part of the conversation at the next table. I was only mildly interested then, but I felt it might be helpful to know more about it for future reference.

The woman at the next table shared with me not only her book but her knowledge of the Bromberg area, which as it turned out was located in Posen in East Germany. She was pleasant but very insistent that I accompany her to the card catalogue where the German records were located. She was so accommodating that I felt it would be unkind not to accept her offer. Upon concluding her explanation of the German records, she turned to me and said, "You really need to talk with Brother Rudolph Noss,

18

the German consultant," and she waved her hand in his direction.

Not wanting to appear rude, I began to explain that I had prepared to work only on my own research on this trip and had not even brought my husband's records. But immediately I sensed it was of no use to explain. She was so enthusiastic — perhaps she was right! It could do no harm to talk with Brother Noss, I concluded. So I allowed myself to be swept along to the desk of the German consultant.

Brother Noss was a delightful person with a silver-grey fringe of hair, twinkling eyes, and a fascinating German accent. After a few moments of conversation in which he was equally as insistent as my new friend, I splurged my last fifteen cents of the day's allowance for a xerox copy of the Julius Harris (of Fordon, Prussia) and Pauline Baer family record and returned it to Brother Noss. Grasping the sheet in his hand, he suddenly became very excited.

"Ah, Bromberg!" he said, as he expertly pulled out a series of maps and catalogues (like a magician with a new rabbit pulled from his hat).

"Thirty-nine films on Bromberg," he pronounced, "and seven more on Fordon!"

"Come, I will show you how to find it," and off we went to the film cabinet, my protests and excuses falling soundlessly to the floor as we walked. Quickly he extracted a church film record of the early 1800s and we hurried to one of the microfilm readers. I tried to explain that I was unable to read German, but he waved aside my poor protest as not worthy of consideration and rolled the film onto the machine. Quickly he reeled to the index at the back A, B, D— no, too far, back to B, down the list of names we read till we came to *Pauline Agathe Beyer* pg. . . . . Brother Noss beamed and turned the record over to me to finish reading.

There was a difference in the spelling, but could it be? Her parents would be mentioned! My hands fumbled as I turned the crank and viewed the film, page after page, until I reached the correct one named in the index. The words of German script appeared strange and the numbers seemed to have odd shapes, yet they were flowing and graceful. Age had not heightened the clarity of the record before me, however. Oh, was I to be led this far and then find the record impossible to read? Suddenly, letter by letter, it became clear: *Pauline Agathe Beyer.*

Again Brother Noss appeared, his twinkling eyes sending a message of "See, I told you it was worth it!" I felt a spirit of love and testimony near me as I continued to search into the records of the past, as Brother Noss had instructed me to do. It was not long, however, before it became apparent that I had reached a language barrier; some of the words and phrases were almost unintelligible to me. How could I make a true and correct record under these circumstances?

Bowing my head in prayer, I sought for the answer from the Lord. I waited in faith, knowing that my prayer would be answered. Then came the still, small voice:

"Diane. Do not fear being alone. You shall be able to read the language if you will listen to my voice which will guide you.

"You are going far across the mountains to a new land, through the mists of the valleys and forth to the villages of my people. Distant lands shall become close and you shall hear the voices of my people echoing across the hillsides, through the valleys and over the mountains to help you. Their hearts are with you in the work you are doing and their prayers follow your efforts. Do not despair, but listen, listen, and you will hear!

"Through the mists of time will their spirits come forth to lead you, if you are humble. Open your heart to me and know that I am able to do all things. Even so. Amen."

Tears started down my face and it was as if for an instant I could see the beautiful mountains and misted valleys and I felt comforted, feeling the love and closeness of these people. My only clean piece of paper was a worn sheet of tracing paper which I used to quickly jot down the message I had just received.

Within a very short time the records became easier to read. Across the aisle a little grey-haired German lady spoke up. Sister Oehlke was also reading films for the German-Posen area and was delighted to know that she and I had people in the same location. She very kindly offered to help me with any problems that arose. Indeed, the Lord had answered my prayer. I had a new friend as well as being able to more easily decipher the German script.

After returning home to Whittier, however, and ordering films at the Los Angeles Temple Library, I became aware of another problem — time! There would not be sufficient time to read each film while it was on loan from Salt Lake City, study the language, and travel across town through traffic for an hour each way to the Temple Library as well as care for my family and Church responsibilities.

While praying about what to do, now that I had gained a deep testimony of this German work, I felt impressed to hire a researcher who would be proficient in the language. Yet how would I pay one? I did not know how, but I felt that the Lord could provide the way. I looked forward to my next trip to Salt Lake, during which time I hoped somehow to make suitable arrangements for the Harris-Baer research.

Arriving in Salt Lake a few months later, I went first to the Genealogical Library. The first person I met there was Sister Oehlke! Her clear blue eyes and silver-grey hair were so pretty, yet I loved her most of all for her sweet spirit. We were happy to see one another and greeted each other warmly. We reviewed again the previous spiritual blessings I had received regarding the Bromberg films, then I related to her my problems of time and money. Without answering, she turned to her quiet, grey-haired lady friend who had been silently standing by her side. They conversed together enthusiastically in the German language for a few moments. Then Sister Oehlke smiled and chirped in a happy voice, "She will do it."

I was taken aback. "Do what?" I asked, not sure exactly what had taken place.

21

"She will read your microfilms for you," beamed Sister Oehlke. She then introduced her friend as Sister Louise Rother, who had arrived only three weeks previously from Hamburg. Sister Rother smiled as we shook hands, then said with a wink of her eye and in her soft German accent, "The dead don't charge." (Sister Oehlke translated.)

"Oh, but Sister Oehlke, I have no money to pay her. I would not have her work without pay. I could perhaps do babysitting and earn the money for her to read one film each week. By the end of the year we could finish the Bromberg films," I concluded.

Sister Oehlke explained my proposal to Sister Rother, who agreed to the plan. I gave her what small amount of information I possessed (one precious sheet) and we exchanged addresses and made ready to part. I felt extremely grateful that my prayers were being answered, and I left Salt Lake at the end of the week with a joyful heart.

I later found Sister Rother to be something other than the quiet, unassuming little lady I had at first thought her to be. She had been hired by the Genealogical Society as a German translator and was an *excellent* researcher. What luck! Yet I knew it was much more than mere luck that had brought us together.

One morning, some thirty days after my return home to California, I heard the slap of the mail upon the entry-way tile and knew by the sound that something special was there. Leaving my tasks, I hurried down the hall to the front door. There among the letters was a small 5" x 8" cream-colored envelope made of a sheet of folded manila paper. It was tied with a simple string, and the writing on it was small and delicate yet perfectly formed. My heart rushed into my throat as I read the return address: S. Louise Rother, Salt Lake City, Utah.

Hurriedly I tore open the envelope. My hand shook as I lifted out a small, homemade notebook of folded graph paper filled with hundreds of German names and dates; a family (husband, wife, children, and grandparents) on each page for some 75 pages! A folded sheet of black paper formed the cover of this precious book and a white paper label taped to the front proclaimed it, "The Family Record of W. R. Deputy."

Overwhelmed, I realized that Sister Rother must have read all thirty-six films on Bromberg in one month!

That very day I began the task of carefully entering the family names and dates of each page on family group sheets. By evening I had compiled quite a number on work sheets. Though very tired as I lay down that night, I experienced a feeling of great satisfaction and joy. As my eyes closed and I began to dream, suddenly I saw a bright light in the shape of a circle. (Almost as if it were a window into a different sphere.) In the center of the circle of light shone the face of a woman who smiled down at me. Her face wore an expression of joy and happiness. I saw her for only an instant and then did not see her again, but I remember well her hair of silver grey, her broad but regal face showing maturity and wisdom, and her expression of happiness, which gave a sparkle to her eyes.

Not many days later I received in the mail a picture of Pauline Baer Harris, whose countenance matched that of the regal lady of my dream. The picture was sent to me by another great-grand-daughter of Pauline's, Vivian Kokalias of San Francisco. At the time she was not aware of the research being conducted for the Baer-Harris family. These circumstances were an added testimony to me of the truthfulness of the work I was engaged in.

My next problem was, How would I ever pay for this great amount of research that had been accomplished? I confided this problem to my husband and we agreed that it would only be possible to pay her small amounts over a long period of time. We felt discouraged.

The next day, however, we were in for a surprise. We received twenty-five dollars a day, three days in a row, from an unexpected source. Three days from then we had the money to pay Sister Rother for her long and arduous hours on the Baer-Harris research.

This may seem like the end of the story, but I would like to add one more event that happened about a month later. The mailman stood at my door with a package in his outstretched hand. As I took it I could at once see that the flimsy outside paper was torn in several places and the string had slipped, yet inside was a large package of family record sheets in perfect condition. Not a corner was bent or marred in any way. I had the distinct impression at that moment that an unseen messenger also stood at my door and safely handed those sheets to me, and I felt the Spirit in great power.

Excitedly I opened the package and found over two hundred typewritten finished sheets ready to be submitted to the Genealogical Society for temple work. They had been compiled by Sister Louise Rother on the Baer-Harris lines.

I was very thankful, but I had one concern. With so many similar names, how would I know whether all the details were correct? I prayed for a confirmation of the Spirit on this, and for three nights I was awakened and each time given the name of a different village or town in Posen. I would then get up and write it down. This in turn helped me identify a particular sheet with that place name. As I would study that sheet, an obvious error on it would come to light. This happened three times and then no more. I then felt an assurance that the records were complete and correct.

The greatest blessing of all came when the names arrived at the Los Angeles Temple for processing and for the ordinance work to be completed. My husband Wally and I were able to do many of the endowments and family sealings for his people. We had the privilege of participating in two complete sealing sessions of approximately five-hundred Baer-Harris, Pryzinski, and other related names, and we felt the joy that comes in service for loved ones who are close to the veil. It was indeed a very special blessing for all who participated, one which they will always remember.

II

Guided Circumstances

Question:

Is it possible that my people beyond the veil can create or cause circumstances which will be advantageous to me as I strive to gather their records and see that the vicarious work is performed for them?

The Bamboo Tree

Kenneth M. Palmer

Although my family has never shown any interest in becoming members of the Church and know very little about our reasons for genealogical research, they have always been interested in family history. Thus we had access to fairly extensive records.

Not long after coming to Auckland, New Zealand, my wife and I had a new home built. At the entrance to the home we had planted a small pebble garden. In this garden, which was formed by two brick walls of the house, we had planted several attractive small shrubs. I had the feeling, however, that to really offset these shrubs it was desirable to plant a dwarf bamboo tree against the brick wall. I called the local nursery and asked if they could get me such a plant, but they said they didn't stock bamboo. They advised me to go to a nursery which specialized in bamboos and which was located in the Waitakeries.

This nursery, owned by Mr. and Mrs. Isaacson, had been the subject of a news commentary on a TV program. It contained many hundreds of varieties of bamboo; in fact, it had the most extensive collection in the Southern Hemisphere.

I rang Mr. Isaacson and told him of my needs. He suggested that I come out late that afternoon. My wife and I thought it would be an opportunity to take the family with us. We left in plenty of time, but when we got to the Waitakeries we took a wrong road. By the time we located the bamboo farm it was dark. We drove through the entrance and along a private road for a few yards. When we came to a fork in the road I turned to the right as I could see a light through the bamboos in that direction. To this day my wife states that the sign clearly showed that the way to the owner's home was to the left, but I chose to ignore the sign.

We drove a few yards to where the light was. I got out of the car. It was quite dark; the bamboo was rustling in an eerie way as I walked to the door and knocked on it. It was opened by an elderly woman who I suppose was in her mid-seventies. Her appearance was somewhat disheveled, although she seemed quite bright and alert.

I explained my business to her and she said, "Well, really it is my son, Mr. Isaacson, Jr., that you wish to see. He lives along the other road, the one you didn't take." She apologized for her appearance and said that she had just arrived back from Tauranga. I was immediately interested and asked, "Well, how was the weather in Tauranga today?"

"Oh," she answered, "as a matter of fact, I was not really in Tauranga, but at Te Puke attending a funeral." This interested me even more. She said, "It was for Jim Hetherington."

"How odd," I replied. "He happens to be my second cousin."

She immediately looked most interested and said, "In that case, you must know Tom Tanner."

"I certainly do," I answered. "He is my uncle."

Then she continued, "You must have known . . ." and she mentioned my mother and many of my close relations.

As we talked, I found that my eldest brother Irwin had even stayed with her on one occasion. "Well, Mr. Palmer," she said, "you would be most interested to see this book that I have. It is the account of my family. It is our genealogy and was published privately in 1870." She brought the book to me. It was a book written by a Mr. Fox and contained the family histories not only of the Fox family but of a number of other families, including the Tanner and Heatherington families. These were my own relations!

Mrs. Isaacson was a Quaker, as were my own grandparents and great-grandparents. Needless to say, I was tremendously interested in this book. She said to me, "This book is very precious to me, and I would certainly on no account let anyone have it." I thanked her for the time we had spent, talked with her a little longer, and then went back to the car. I told my wife of the experience and said, "Before long we are going to come back and we are going to get that little book that is so precious to us." We obtained our bamboo from Mrs. Isaacson's son and went home.

Two or three weeks later my wife and I came back. I went to Mrs. Isaacson's house, and when she came to the door she remembered me at once. I told her how interested I was in the family history. After talking for some time I asked her if it might be possible to borrow her book and have it photostated. She said, "Because I knew your mother and your family members, I will gladly let you have the loan of it. I have yet another book which you might also be interested in. This is a record of the Society of Friends."

I was able to borrow both books and have photostats taken. The relevant information was extremely valuable, and as a consequence the work was done in the temple for hundreds of names.

The bamboo plant grew and flourished; in fact, so much that each year it had to be cut back quite considerably.

29

Two Reserved Seats

J. W. Johnson

One morning in the summer of 1968 I told my wife that I was going to spend the day at the Genealogical Library looking for information on some of our family lines. I arrived at the library (then located on Main Street at First South in Salt Lake City) about 10:00 A.M. I worked in the patrons section until about 2:30 P.M. By this time I had had very little success in locating any additional names for our book of remembrance and was getting tired.

Normally I would have gone directly to the parking lot, got in my car, and started for home, but for reasons unknown to me this day I decided to rest for a few minutes before leaving. There were very few patrons in the building at the time; almost all of the desks were empty. I sat down at one that was about six or eight desks from the front door. After about ten minutes a man and two women came in the door and walked directly to the desk where I was sitting. Considering that all the other desks were unoccupied it seemed strange that the man and one of the women should sit directly opposite me while the other woman sat right next to me.

The woman by my side opened a book of remembrance containing some family group sheets. She took some of the sheets out of the book and placed them between us. Being a little nosey and knowing that genealogy shows up in the strangest places, I looked at the top sheet. To my amazement I saw that it was for the family of Thomas Abbott and Bridget Green, my direct ancestors!

I told the lady that I had no idea who she was but that that sheet related to my ancestors. She introduced herself: she was from Smithfield, Utah; she had come to Salt Lake City because she was unable to get interested in anything at home; and she had talked her husband into bringing her to the archives to work on the Abbott line that went into the Nason line.

The Nason line had been of particular concern to me and my sister, Leona Nielsen of Ashland, Oregon. We had done a lot of praying about the line. We had been trying to find something on it for over twenty-five years but because we could not find Aaron Nason we were unable to find any connection with any of the Nason lines in the library. Concluding that the name Aaron Nason must be in error, we had almost given up. We just referred to it as our "ghost line."

This lady from Smithfield was kind enough to show me her records. They proved to be my Nason line. (By now I wasn't tired any more.) I was able to give her eighteen generations on our Goodwin line on which she had been searching for years. I helped her make some corrections on her sheets for the Nason line and also together we were able to submit 139 names for ordinance work to be done in the Logan Temple. The temple work is all done now, and I am sure it was guidance from above that directed her to sit at my desk that day.

On another occasion I went to the Genealogical Library but this time I couldn't find a place to work as all the desks appeared full. Disappointed, I started to leave, but just as I reached the second desk from the door I noticed a vacant seat and sat down.

One of the lines I had been researching in vain was the Wood line. My mother was a Wood and her family line went back to New England to about the time of the Pilgrims; but my sister and I could not find anything tracing the family to England or to any other European country. James Wood and Experience Fuller, my sixth great-grandparents, were as far as we could go. We knew that James Wood's father was Henry Wood, but despite our many prayers we were unable to identify him further, even after reading many histories of New England.

On the occasion I have in mind, as I sat down at the one vacant seat, I noticed on the table a book opened to a sheet for "Henry Atwood or Wood." Surely it was too much to hope that this was my Henry Wood! But it proved correct — Henry Wood's ninth child was James Wood and he had married Experience Fuller. The dates and places were correct.

I forgot about the lines I had intended to work on and spent the rest of the day with my Atwood ancestors. I was then able to extend the line back through Atwood, Attwood, and Atte Wood to Peter de Wychurst, who lived in the House of Wood, or Hoully House, in 1180. All their temple work had been done except for James Wood and Experience Fuller. (She was a descendant of the Mayflower Fullers.)

My wife and I were later able to go through the Salt Lake Temple and complete the endowments for Experience and James Wood and have them sealed to each other and also to their parents. I felt sure they were in the temple when these ordinances were performed for them. This link completed a seven-hundred-year span of the Atwood family. Henry Atwood or Wood was with the Pilgrims when they were in Holland, and he came to America shortly after the Pilgrims crossed the Atlantic on the *Mayflower*.

About two months later I was walking through the Cottonwood Mall in Salt Lake City. I went into the Deseret Book Store for some supplies and noticed that they were having a sale on some of their books. I picked up a book entitled *Searching with Success*. Near the back of the book was the Fuller genealogy that went back to 1422. This was Experience Fuller's line! As a result I have been able to prove that I am a descendant of five of the passengers on the *Mayflower*. Also in this book was my Palmer line that extended my line to the Magna Charta barons.

The West Story

Rellis Van Petty: Part I

I was called as an ordinance worker at the Los Angeles Temple in 1956, and I spent some time working at the baptismal font. That is where I first got acquainted with Squire West. He and I worked at the baptismal font for about a year before we became officiators and ordinance workers upstairs. I was made ordinance supervisor in 1959. Squire served as my assistant for about five years, and we worked closely together during that time. We also associated in the real estate business for about a year and became exceptionally good friends.

Squire moved to St. George and worked in both the St. George Temple and the visitors center for about a year and a half before he died. When he passed on, his wife called me and I went to St. George to help her make all the funeral arrangements.

I was a sealer in the Los Angeles Temple for eight years. One evening about six months after Squire had died, I went to the temple as usual to do my regularly assigned sealings. There were eight sealers working that evening. When we started to divide up the assignments, we found that one of the stakes assigned had not shown up. I suggested to the sealer who had that stake assigned to him that he take my group, and that I would go out to the recommend desk and request volunteers to do the sealing session.

33

I enjoyed requesting help because I had had some beautiful experiences with volunteers. I arrived at the recommend desk just as the deadline arrived for the 6:00 P.M. session. A couple there were trying to persuade the man at the desk to let them in to that session. I overheard them say they had arranged for a babysitter at home in Hawthorne, California, and could not wait for the next session, which was due to begin an hour later.

This man and woman were almost weeping because they felt so badly about missing the session. I put my arms around their shoulders and said: "Now, folks, don't feel so badly. The Lord purposely slowed you down on the freeway so that you could help me on this sealing session." I didn't know at the time how much I really meant that statement.

The couple didn't know what a sealing session was; I told them it would be the greatest experience of their lives, as we were going to seal couples together that night. I had about ninety couples to seal. I told them that if we could get three or four more couples, they would be home at about the same time as if they had attended an endowment session. Needless to say, they were thrilled to think that their time in coming had not been spent in vain.

I handed them a slip of paper and asked them to write down their names, get dressed, and meet me upstairs. They left, and I walked down the corridor to where a lady was holding the door open for her husband who was running up the walkway from the parking area, hoping to catch the 6:00 P.M. session. It only took a minute to convince them to help me with the sealing session rather than wait an hour for the next endowment session. They were thrilled, as they had not had the experience of working in a sealing session. I took their names and instructed them as I had the other couple, then I went to my locker and changed into my white suit.

By the time I came back there were about twenty-four couples in the waiting room who had missed the six o'clock session. I asked for four volunteers. One couple who was sitting part of the way back stood up; they said they would be glad to participate. Another couple from Orem, Utah, sitting on the front row, also volunteered.

This Utah couple was on vacation and had just come from a visit to Marineland. On the freeway they had spotted the temple spire and decided to visit the temple grounds. At about 4:00 P.M. they got back on the Santa Monica freeway to return to Marineland, but the heavy late-afternoon Los Angeles traffic changed their minds and they decided to rent a room in a nearby motel and return to the temple for a session.

The Utah couple put their names on the paper and went to dress. I took the papers and started filling out my cards. Suddenly I felt the Spirit like a shock of electricity, and at first I couldn't discern what it was. I liked the feeling and just drank it in for a couple of minutes. Then I noticed that three of the four names of the couples was West. At first I thought it was quite a coincidence, but then I realized that the Lord wanted them here on this sealing. I felt that Squire was somehow maneuvering this!

As I wrote those names on the cards I almost gloated over the knowledge I had. If those people didn't know each other, this was going to be a marvelous experience.

As the nine of us entered the sealing room I laid my paperwork on the chair and asked, "Who is Brother Rowley?" He was the young man who had left his children with the babysitter. I walked over and shook hands with him and said, "I'm Brother Petty, and you and I are strangers here tonight." I told him that the other folks were all related, as they all had the last name of West. An astonished look came over all their faces. They couldn't believe it. They thought I was kidding but I assured them I was not. I told them that a relative of the Wests used to work there in the temple, and that I suspected he had had something to do with this. At this point Brother Rowley said, "My wife's maiden name was West."

Everyone felt the presence of the Spirit in that room. There were tears in everyone's eyes. When the Lord does something like

35

that he doesn't make any mistakes, and suddenly it came to the understanding of the eight people that the Lord had had something to do with getting each one of them there. The way things had happened during the day, it seemed that some of them had almost missed coming, and that there was almost no other way to go but the routes they took.

After we talked a bit we decided that one of them had met Squire West in the Los Angeles Temple while he was officiating there and found that they were related to him. I told them about Squire and my affiliation with him.

We finally settled down to the sealing session and sealed ninety couples. In the sealings the name Maria West came up three times, and everyone present recognized it as a family name. All four couples had done genealogical research. We sealed thirty-two couples with the surname of West that night. Spiritual influences aside, one would have sworn I had gone through a million computer sheets to get those West names. The thing that makes it more unusual is that I had traded packets with the man who was supposed to have done that sealing session. All I did apart from that was to take a block of names out of my original packet, because the other man didn't want to do the larger number of sealings, and add them to my new packet.

Audrey West Oliver: Part II

My lifelong quest has been to find genealogical information about my grandfather, Robert Lee West of Georgia, who was killed when my father, Ben Lee West, was two years old.

As a child I visited in Kentucky quite often before coming to California and got to know my father's mother and the other side of the family. But the missing person I really wanted to know about was my grandfather, Robert Lee West. He was a policeman in Hopkinsville, Kentucky, when my father was two years old. He was shot by a policeman on the force who had been suspended for actions unbecoming to a policeman and who took out his resentment on my grandfather. That left my father fatherless and worked a hardship on his family (his mother, his sister Alice, and himself).

Whenever I asked about my grandfather I was given evasive explanations. Nothing was ever told me about him, but I had absorbed the knowledge that he had been married once before he married my grandmother. A child by his first wife had died and the marriage had subsequently been dissolved. That was all I knew about my grandfather.

I did have a few other bits of related information — some names of cousins of my father and a wedding announcement from my grandfather's brother in Sardis, Mississippi, announcing the marriage of his daughter Aline. I knew too that the family had moved to Charleston, Mississippi. The wedding announcement listed my grandfather's brother as John Quinn West, so I knew then the name of one of the brothers. I also remembered hearing something about Joe and James, but I didn't know just who they were. I have heard that I met my cousins as a little girl, but all contact was lost when we came to California, where my father was killed in a motorcycle accident when I was fifteen. Mother, Daisy Tieman West, then raised my brother Cort, my sister Vivian, and myself.

As my grandmother Mary Vaughan West knew nothing about the West side of the family, after we moved I received no information about my father's folks. I had heard there was a West home in Georgia that was supposed to be still standing. There were some unidentified photos of men who supposedly were my grandfather's brothers, but there were no names on them so I could not be certain. When it came down to the information I had, I believed my grandfather had been born near Macon, Georgia, and I had the wedding announcement from 1915 which gave the name of my grandfather's brother from Sardis, Mississippi.

Later, I had a friend who went to Georgia. Her husband was stationed there and I asked her to try to locate the West family in Macon, Georgia. She wrote letters, telephoned, and did everything she could, but the West families in Macon all denied any connection with the family. I had reached another dead end.

Several years after my mother passed away on November 2, 1970, I dreamed of a big, beautiful southern home. In my dream it was almost dark outside and there was a light inside the home. I walked up to the house, and I thought, "They won't mind me looking around." I went around to the back and looked in. In the center of the hall was a beautiful crystal chandelier shining brilliantly, and I could see the entrance at the front door. I returned to the front. I don't recall really looking in as I had at the back, but I could see the light inside.

As I stood looking at the home, I said to myself, "I wonder who this home belongs to!" And then right across the front of the home appeared big blazoned letters which read "West." Then I knew I had found my home and the home of my grandparents.

I knew that someday if I could return to Georgia I would find that home. But it couldn't be in Macon, so I knew there had to be some more developments. In June 1974 I asked Diane Deputy to assist me with the West research, as she was doing research on the other side of the family. She wrote letters for me to mail to Sardis, Mississippi, and Macon, Georgia, still the only two clues I had. But as I was too ill to mail the letters, they were postponed.

When I got better the letters were finally mailed. I waited for an answer but nothing came back. Not even the letters were returned, so I knew I had reached another dead end. In the meantime I told Diane I had received no answers. Meantime, on her own she had run across part of the line and the name Reverend John Quinn West, the same name as that on the wedding announcement.

But once again I was stopped, as we could not find exactly where the family connected, although we knew we had hit the right family line. It had to be an offshoot as it wasn't the direct line and contained no familiar names other than Reverend John Quinn West of Wilkes County, Georgia.

Since my father died I have always been aware of his love and protection, and in times of danger I have felt he has always been with me. I have known it because he has been so real to me. A year or so ago, one night just a few days before my father's birthday I had a dream about him. He asked, "What are you doing to help Diane find the West family?" As I hadn't been involved, I had to answer, "Nothing." He admonished, "You get busy and help Diane with the work of finding the Wests."

As I woke up I thought: "What can I do? I have nowhere to start." I felt impressed to search again through the boxes of Mother's things as I had done before. I picked the first box and opened it. I remembered having looked through it before, but this time I opened a booklet and found several pages from the West family Bible, vital papers which listed my grandfather Robert Lee's birth in Stewart County, Georgia, in 1847, his brother's birth, and so forth. There were dates of births, marriages, and deaths; and though some dates were incomplete, enough information was there to enable us to find out more about the West family.

I wrote to Stewart County, Georgia. A judge answered my letter and said that all he had on file were three West wills. One will was for Mary A. West and it was recorded in 1855; one for William West, 1874; and the third for Fort West, a cousin, 1885.

When I opened the copy of the wills the names were unfamiliar because I did not then know the name of Robert Lee West's father. It seemed like another dead end. I decided to send the three wills to Diane to see what she could do. She started checking and found that Mary A. West was my great-great-grandmother. Hers was the first will and the oldest. The second will was that of William West who was Robert Lee West's uncle. We didn't research Fort West. We had all we needed. Diane then tied it all together and then found the rest of the information needed to prove the West line.

What a revelation it was to open the booklet and find those vital papers which I never knew existed! Mother had not known they existed either. They had just been shoved away because they were old and supposedly of little value. Daddy having been dead so long, apparently Mother thought no one would want to know much about his family, but I did. I had been searching from the time I was a child to learn of my family. I had to decipher the records on the family Bible pages because some of the entries were pretty hard to read. Then I received from Diane the census records, newspaper articles of Kentucky deaths and marriages, marriage bonds, and histories which added much to my knowledge of the Wests.

We were very fortunate that the records and wills had not been destroyed, because Georgia had suffered much fire and devastation in the Civil War. I feel it was the result of inspiration that things opened up as they did, and that God took a hand in it. I feel that Dad came back again because he wanted his children to know his family too, and he knew how much I had always longed to know.

I am not a member of The Church of Jesus Christ of Latter-day Saints, but I am nevertheless appreciative of its family research program. I am grateful that my ancestors can be sealed in the temple. I'm sure they approve.

Diane Dreier Deputy: Part III

I first remember the name West as a little girl, going with my parents to visit Aunt Daisy West and her children, Audrey, Cort and Vivian. Daisy's husband, Ben, had died shortly after I was born.

Mother has often spoken to me about the day Uncle Ben came to visit, the same day he was fatally injured in a motorcycle accident. She has always remembered his cheerful spirit and his loving ways. It is strange, but we have always felt a closeness to him through all these years.

Our family has been close in some ways, although we have

40

been separated by many miles and consequently have not shared a great many things. When Aunt Daisy passed away in 1970, I attended the funeral in California. Since I was the only member of the Church in my family at that time, I prepared the records for the temple work to be done for her. I made the decision to have her sealed to her parents and to her husband, Ben Lee West.

I traveled from Utah to the Los Angeles Temple to participate in this sealing. Rellis V. Petty was officiating as the sealer that night. Since I had been a scribe in the temple for six years while I lived in the Los Angeles area, I knew Brother Petty very well. That night we did the sealings for my two aunts, Daisy and Gladys (who had passed away within a two-month period), but the name West was not mentioned because at that time my aunts were sealed only to their parents, William Edward Tieman and Susanna Bolin.

That evening Brother Petty told me his part of the West story. (I appreciated its significance, and he agreed to share it with the readers of this book. See Part I of the West story.)

Returning to Utah I was surprised to find a letter from my first cousin, Audrey West Oliver, asking if I would consider trying to find for her some information about her father's family. Since Audrey was unaware of my California visit and the sealing of her mother which had just taken place, I considered this a very significant and inspired request. Despite heavy pressures on my time, I wanted to help her out of love for the family. I felt a strong spirit as I answered her letter to this effect and told her I would not accept payment for this research.

Soon a letter arrived from her with an old wedding announcement and some other bits of information she had been able to gather — the sum total of her findings. The announcement of a Sardis, Mississippi, wedding was dated 1915. The bride's father was named John Quinn West, an uncle of her father, Ben West.

At the Genealogical Library a few days later I felt impressed to proceed to the Georgia section. Arriving there I studied my

41

papers for a moment, then reached for a book on Georgia Baptists. Finding no index references for another patron's surnames I was working on, I replaced the book. Strange that that inspired choice had revealed nothing! Just then a small quiet voice said to me, "Try West," so I went back to the book. It just seemed to fall open to the page containing the name John Quinn West. He was of a much earlier time period than the one on the announcement, having been born in 1800 in Wilkes County, Georgia, and was a Baptist minister.

While I did not know his relationship, the Spirit strongly testified to me that this gentleman was part of the family. I was on the right track! I xeroxed the information. Since I only had about forty-five minutes, I quickly searched the Wilkes County indexes of cemetery records, wills, probates, marriage records, and so forth, and took the information home.

I was awakened that night with a strong impression to continue working on the West genealogy. At 3:00 A.M. I wrote a long letter to Audrey and included the copies I had made. As I prayed I was also inspired about what kind of genealogical correspondence to include for Audrey to mail, and where she should send those inquiries.

Some time passed with no response from Audrey, then I found that she had been ill. Months passed, then she wrote confirming my fears that her adversities were blurring the importance of the research. I kept praying for her.

After many months had passed, I had a dream of Audrey. She looked fairly well. As she stood before me smiling she had some letters in her hand. When I looked down at them, however, they were very small, about two or three inches square, and there was *nothing* in those letters. I tried to open one but could not.

I wrote Audrey and told her of the dream about the letters. She replied and indicated to me that she was feeling better and that she now intended to mail the letters I had prepared for her to send. (That was the first I knew they had not been mailed.)

42

No answer was ever received from those letters. When I didn't hear any more from Audrey I didn't know what to do. I decided that if she really wanted to find her ancestors she would get at it; otherwise I would have to drop the West research. We went through Christmas and then into the first part of 1976.

One day I received from Audrey through the mail some pages from the West family Bible containing death and birth records, names, dates, and all kinds of extremely important information. There was even a picture of some of the Wests. I was greatly surprised because I had thought Audrey had discontinued the project. This packet contained the Bible records she had found.

Her letter told me that her father had come to her in a dream, and told her to "get busy." This was when she found the Bible records. (See Part II of this story.) To me that letter was a thrilling testimony that even though her father had died when I was two months old, he knew me very well, and that the love I felt for him was certainly generated by his love for me all these years. That testimony brought me great joy.

I read through the Bible records and determined that Audrey's grandfather was born in Georgia in Stewart County in 1847. The obvious step now was to search the 1850 census for that area. On my next visit to the library I was working on some other records and did not even have time for a census search. Nevertheless the impression came to me to search the 1850 census of Stewart County. I had only about twenty minutes left. By the time I located the film and put it on the machine I had only five minutes in which to find the family. I told Heavenly Father that that was all the time I had and that he was going to have to help me! Sure enough I was able to quickly find the family of Robert West's parents, John and Nancy West, and the children, including Robert, age three. I also found the name of a woman, Mary A. West, who I suspected was the mother, but I could not prove it at that time.

On another day I saved a few minutes to work on the West line and found a history of Stewart County, Georgia. In it was a story of Mary A. West, wife of John West of Wilkes County. There were a number of references to the Wests, including a picture of the southern mansion of the West family. This picture was very, very close to the description Audrey gave of the West mansion in her dream. It was a testimony to both of us of the reality of the dream.

Searching in the Wilkes County records I found the will of John West of Wilkes County, naming his wife Mary and all of his six children. This took the line back to the late 1700s. The next prompting of the Spirit suggested a recheck of the archives. There I found a family group sheet of John M. West and Mary M. Quinn, the daughter of John Quinn. I realized that the first day I had gone to the library and had been prompted to look in the Georgia book where I found the story of John Quinn West was indeed very significant, because John Quinn West was the key word to open the line, and it named the ancestors who came into Georgia. There were two, actually — John Quinn and John West. The combination *John Quinn West* was made up of the two surnames brought together. By following that I was able to take the line back about four generations.

I know that the West family beyond the veil is very receptive to the gospel for I feel their love and helpful spirit. They have accepted the gospel and want to progress on. They will help anyone who is receptive at all; and because I was a researcher and a member of the Church and able to work with Audrey, it helped to open her line. Any work that I have been able to do has been done with a minimum amount of effort and a maximum amount of inspiration. I had not always intended to work on the West's genealogy, but the Spirit was very, very strong in guiding me to whatever reference needed to be found. The line opened very quickly once it began. There was no hesitation, and it was just one step after another, as quickly as I could work.

Another interesting sidelight occurred in the latter part of 1976. A group of women came from California to do genealogical research in Salt Lake City. As we were visiting together, Audrey West Oliver and myself and close friends of many years, we discovered that two others of the group also have West lines and have felt impressed to work on them — and so the West story continues.

My Face Beams

John Van Weezep

A few years ago a member of the Church from Hawaii came to the Genealogical Library where I am employed as a consultant in the European section. After examining certain sealing records he had come to see, he came to my office in tears and told me this story:

When he was a child he and his family went to the temple to be sealed. He remembered the sealing very well. In the last couple of nights, however, he had had a strange dream about this sealing. He had seen himself as a child again, back in the temple with his family. They were sitting together in one of the halls. Finally the door to the sealing room opened and the sealer called them all in, *except* his two younger sisters.

This man could not understand why he had this dream, which occurred two nights in succession. He thought that surely there must be some significance to the dream. Could there be something he did not understand about the sealing of his family? "Why were my two sisters to stay *outside* the sealing room?" he had asked himself. "We were *all* sealed."

When he came to my office, tears were streaming down his cheeks. He had found the family group sheet and discovered that his two sisters had not in fact been sealed! Clearly that sealing would be his first priority.

46

To me, this is the way the Spirit works — as a revealer of truths heretofore unknown. I have witnessed it many times.

On one occasion a man came to me and said, "Brother Van Weezep, I have been held up on my line for twenty years. For the past eight years I have been a bishop and have not been actively working on my genealogy, but suddenly I want to work on it once more."

"What seems to be the problem?" I asked. "Won't you sit down, and we'll see what we can do."

To make a really long story short, I looked at the family name and said: "I'm sure there must be more to it than what you've uncovered thus far. That name sounds familiar to me. Let me check in the books."

I found records on his own grandparents and "broke the line wide open clear back" (as the expression goes among those of us who research).

A week or so later he came to me and said, "Brother Van Weezep, may I talk with you? I want to tell you more of my experience."

"Eight years ago when I was made a bishop, I was promised in the blessing given me when I was ordained that if I would concentrate all my attention on my new assignment as a bishop, toward the end of my tenure as a bishop my genealogical line would be wide open. Recently I brought my line to your attention and you solved it. It was indeed broken wide open, and last Sunday I was released as a bishop."

To others this might seem coincidental, but to a member of the Church it is not a coincidence. This is the way the Spirit works.

Genealogical research is my life's work. Through a blessing given to me by my stake patriarch I learned that the people in the hereafter were petitioning the Lord to show me where the records are so that I may be an instrument in his hands to see that their work is done.

It is uncanny the way that information falls into my lap. While I was in Holland, representing the Genealogical Society in Holland, Belgium, and Luxembourg, I was checking into the various records available for microfilming and into the possibility of obtaining permission to microfilm.

I went to an archive and introduced myself. The archivist interrupted me, saying: "Oh, we have a book here that was just published which might interest you. It deals with the area your family came from." I looked at the book and saw the names of my third great-grandparents and also of my Scottish grandmother. I already had this information, but I bought the book for the Society. After I returned home and had time to open it again, I found the names of my ninth, eighth, seventh, and so on, down to fourth great-grandparents, as well as all the extensions I did not already have.

The author of the book and I had a difference of opinion about my eighth and ninth great-grandparents. I wrote to an office in Holland for which I am a foreign correspondent, and they responded that they could not find a complete genealogy on the family. I was sitting at my desk one day after I had received the disappointing letter. After twenty-two years with the Society, I thought I knew all the material in the library, but I guess I still don't. Suddenly I said to my co-worker, "I have to go to the Q section, because there is a book I need."

I went down there and fell on my knees. I saw the book. In it was the whole family I had been searching — pictures of my eighth great aunt and uncle, pictures of their sons, and one who was a very famous preacher. It was the first page I turned to! Afterward I learned that the person who wrote the book died a short while before I found it. This may all be coincidental, but not to me.

The feeling of closeness to those beyond the veil is indescribable. These souls are near and dear to me, especially when I go into the temple and sit in the sealer's chair. I was the assistant temple recorder for fourteen years. Now I am a sealer and have that authority. When I know that I am sealing my ninth great-grandparents, my eighth, seventh, and so on, I recognize that they are the ones who brought me forth and now I can return the favor by doing the work for them. As I repeat the promises and blessings, only one who does it can know how I feel.

A lot of people say that we are working for the dead but we are not — we are working for the living. They are alive in an eternal sense, and they are aware of much more than we are. They know much more than we do; for one thing, they know what we are doing but we don't know what they are doing. They are much more *alive* than we. They are waiting for us. They pray, they petition our Father in heaven that we may be inspired in our research work. What would be the purpose of this whole life we have to go through if there is nothing beyond? For what reason would we be receiving the inspiration which we do? Why would we be guided to do all this work if there is no hereafter? In my humble testimony, I know they are alive.

At the time when I started to work on my German line I did not know that I was also Scottish. My grandfather was a military doctor. I could not find him anywhere, except that I knew where he died. I did everything I could. I searched everywhere. I finally said, "I'm going to leave them alone and they will have to let *me* know where they are. I have too many lines to worry about. *They* will have to come across themselves."

About a year and one-half later I suddenly felt the urge to work on the line again. I believe these "urges" are inspired, because mine always end in good results. I said, "It's time to work on the Kinsbach line." Right away I found two people with whom I could correspond. I found that it is a Scottish line and it is now documented back to my tenth great-grandparents, to the twelfth century. I know our people are working with us. We just have to give them time to get ready, I guess.

49

This work is almost an obsession with me. I feel I *have* to get the names to the temple. When I find a name on my line — a person whose identity has not been proven to me before — I light up, and my wife knows I have identified another person on the line. I have been blessed to do the temple work for over a thousand people. I know that this great work is truly of the Lord, and my face beams when I have been privileged to contribute to it.

Ripples into Eternity

Linda Monk Dursteler

Early in the year 1975, circumstances in our household began to go awry. My husband and I were expecting our fifth child when my remarkably good health began to fail. There was no detectable medical reason for the problems that afflicted me. The doctor tried various remedies, but nothing helped. Then my father-in-law was stricken with a heart attack, had a stroke and died.

One week to the hour after the funeral of our father, our son was born. Three days later it was discovered that he was born with some serious infections. Specialists were called in, but they told us that there was nothing more that could be done for him; they held little hope that the baby would live through the night.

The baby was immediately administered to and given a name and blessing. The next morning I left the hospital, having never heard my little son cry, leaving him barely alive in the intensive care unit. Through all of this my husband was out of state a great deal, still trying to comfort his mother and get her affairs in order.

Some months before this time I had submitted about a hundred names for temple work. Most were names with whom I could not prove any direct relationship, but I felt that in order to make the book work complete and finish the research these names needed to be submitted. They were all from the ancestral area, and I believed that these people deserved the same privileges as the two or three whom I could prove as direct ancestry. Just prior to my father-in-law's death, I received notification that half of the names had been cleared.

After I returned home from the hospital I received the clearances on the rest of the names. As I picked up the packet to file it away, I was indeed overcome. I was impressed by the spirits of those names. It was as if a voice had spoken to me, telling me, "For what you have done for us, for all your efforts in research and ensuring our temple blessings, we are supporting you, petitioning for you in your troubles."

I have heard many genealogical researchers ask whether or not those people whose names they have researched really do appreciate all the time and effort expended in their behalf. I received my answer to that question. The spirits bore witness to me that *they are eternally grateful and will help us in return*. I was blessed to see my son recover from his near-fatal infections. The blessings from this research work are like a pebble thrown into a lake — the ripples continue on into eternity.

III

Success Through Correspondence

Question:

I do not live near an LDS branch library, nor do I like to write letters. I don't even know where to begin. Do people actually answer genealogical inquiries, or is it a waste of time writing them?

Following Through

James D. MacArthur

The Prophet Joseph Smith once said, "I want to go back to the beginning, and so lift your minds into a more lofty sphere and a more exalted understanding than what the human mind generally aspires to." (N.B. Lundwall, comp., *The Vision*, Bookcraft, page 16.)

Contrary to what the Prophet wanted for us, we seem to associate vagueness and distance with our premortal and postmortal lives. We are in clear touch with earth life, but other aspects of our eternal existence seem too "far away." But I personally know that they are *very* close and that our life here on this earth, though vitally important, is but a moment in eternity. Our helping hands must reach out to those waiting close by in the world of spirits.

Let me share with you just one small instance out of countless which I could describe, that illustrates to me that there are "subtle influences" that may guide us in our efforts to reach out and provide an opportunity for our kindred families to be possessors of the sacred ordinances of the gospel of Jesus Christ.

About two years ago I made an effort to contact my mother, a Catholic, and learn something of her family. She told me a lamentable story regarding her youth and family experiences.

55

In 1918 when my mother was about six years old she lost her father during the flu epidemic. He was only thirty-one and left a widow and three small children. Grandmother took Mother and the other two children back home to Michigan to live for a while where family members were available to help.

Tragedy was not new to Grandma, for she had also been a fatherless baby. Her father was killed at the age of twenty-nine. My grandmother's real mother, according to court records, was left totally destitute and could not care for her only daughter. My grandmother was then adopted by a wonderful couple named William Nellis and Rose Lucia Thibeau. He was of German ancestry and she was French. My heart went out to this selfless couple as I viewed pictures of them holding my own mother after the death of her young father, and as I heard how they had lovingly raised my grandmother to maturity. I then decided that somehow I must not only learn more about these great people but I *must* see that they would have an opportunity to accept the sacred ordinances of the gospel that could be performed for them in the Lord's house.

As is not uncommon, however, I immediately had difficulty with my task. No one was alive that knew them or anything about them except my mother, who only had fond memories — no records regarding their birth, death, or any other significant events.

I made the assumption that possibly, though they adopted my grandmother, their names and places of birth *might* be on my grandmother's birth record from the state of Wisconsin. I wrote to Wisconsin and was thrilled when the birth certificate returned, listing the adoptive parents and their places of birth! My joy turned to gloom shortly, however, when attempt after attempt failed to verify their dates and places of birth.

I finally focused my efforts on my great-grandmother Thibeau, as apparently she was born in the United States and my great-grandfather was not. Nevertheless, my efforts to verify her birth in Wisconsin in the 1860s proved continually fruitless. I tried everything, including writing to libraries and placing public notices in newspapers near her place of birth, to no avail.

I became discouraged, and I was prepared to assume that for some reason the time was not right for this work to be accomplished. I blamed myself for "leaving some key unturned" that would help me bless my great-grandmother — she who had selflessly given so much to our family in adopting and raising my grandmother!

I suddenly had an inclination to walk over to the BYU Genealogical Library at noon and visit with a friend who works in that program to see what he might suggest. After a brief review of my efforts he just shook his head, at a loss to suggest much else I could do. Just before I left he had a sudden idea that I might try writing to the Wisconsin State Genealogical Society to see if any members were working on the Thibeau line.

As I left, I decided against this "long shot." I did not welcome another failure. A few days later, however, I felt impelled to do as he had suggested. What could I lose? What might I gain!

I sent off a letter to the State Genealogical Society in Wisconsin, asking for the names and addresses of anyone working on the surname of Thibeau. To my delight and surprise, I soon received a response from the society, indicating that in their list of members they could locate only *one* individual who had worked on that surname, though it was a fairly common French surname. The woman's name was Marie T. St. Louis of Shorewood, Wisconsin.

Again I nearly did not follow through. *One* name — what chance could there be that she knew anything about my great-grandmother who was born over one hundred years ago?

But, feeling that if I must fail I would fail only after a complete effort on my part, I wrote to Miss St. Louis. About two weeks passed and no response came. I concluded the address was wrong or she could not help me. Anyhow, my long struggle was over!

About a week later a package came in the mail from Wisconsin! I quickly opened it and came very close to becoming a twenty-nine-year-old heart-attack case when I saw its contents!

In an enclosed letter this dear woman apologized for taking so long to answer my request. She was elderly, lived alone, and could not drive a car. In order to make copies of her own records she had to mail them to a local library for printing and have them mailed back.

She had been interested in family research for about six years, she wrote. She then stated, "Your great-grandmother, Rose Thibeau, and my mother are sisters." She proceeded to write that she had had unusually good luck in tracing Thibeau and related family lines back to about 1480! Enclosed were about 100 entire family group sheets, and she indicated she had about 150 more she would send if I could pay the printing costs!

To put it mildly, I was breathless! After finally receiving all the group sheets she had to send me, I calculated that this great soul had sent information on about two thousand members of my family and had now opened the door for me to not only bless my great-grandmother and her family but myriads of others who were all one great family.

During the month of September 1974, my great-grandmother Thibeau, all of her brothers and sisters, and her parents were baptized, endowed, and sealed by proxy work in the Provo Temple. In the months to follow, ordinance work was accomplished for many others as I continued my effort to do the needed work for all my family in the Lord's house. On one evening, my wife and I sealed seventeen children to my fifth great-grandparents in this great family!

This is *not* a miracle. It happens when we truly desire to serve and extend our love beyond the veil into the world of spirits. Many there wait for the key that unlocks the door to the presence of their Father. We hold that key.

58

I am personally convinced that our premortal state, mortality, and our postmortal existence are simply one continuum. The work of God goes on in all phases of it.

I pray we may understand that teaching the gospel to those who did not know it in this life is a work done in the spirit world that we mortals cannot do; but temple ordinance work for those who are dead can only be done *here* on the earth, and *only* we, you and I, can do it!

May we be selfless, as was my wonderful great-grandmother, and devote ourselves to reaching beyond the veil where *they* wait for us!

(Compilers' note: James David MacArthur joined the Church in 1962 at seventeen years of age. He has completed his B.A., M.A., and Ph.D. degrees since his marriage in 1968, and in those same eight years the MacArthurs have been blessed with eight children, including two sets of twins. From 1973 to 1976 they completed about seven hundred temple ordinances for Brother MacArthur's family. At Brigham Young University Brother MacArthur is Chairman of the Department of Academic Standards and Assistant Director of the Personal and Career Assistance Program. He is thirty-one years old.)

Catherine Gulick

Sylvia Thatcher

Catherine Gulick, Catherine Gulick, Catherine Gulick — I tried to think other thoughts, but I would soon find the same name running over and over like a record stuck in one place.

Catherine Gulick was my husband's third great-grandmother, married to Joseph Kitchen of New Jersey. That was all my husband and I knew about her. Members of the family had tried unsuccessfully to locate her parents. I felt I was too busy with my own genealogy to take on my husband's. When her name came into my mind, I would try to force it out by thinking of other things. After about six months of fighting this, I gave up. I decided to put forth some small effort on behalf of Catherine.

The easiest thing I could think of was to run an ad in a genealogical newspaper and inquire concerning Catherine Gulick. This I did and was then able to find some peace of mind.

To my surprise I soon received a letter from an elderly lady whose maiden name had been Helen Gulick. She lived within twenty miles of me! She wrote that she had Gulick genealogical data back to 1675, or thereabouts. Her father had worked forty years on the Gulick and allied families, and she had also worked on the lines for about the same length of time. She had not only her records and those of her father, but a copy of a manuscript formerly owned by a New York banker. This gentleman and his brother, both deceased now, had hired professional genealogical researchers for years to search out the Gulicks. There were about one thousand names involved. Helen compiled these records into four looseleaf notebooks, one for each of four Gulick brothers and their ancestors and descendants.

The first time my husband and I visited Helen we were not permitted to see the records. We returned home very disappointed. We decided to fast and pray and then return a second time. Not only did we see her records that time, but Helen suggested I take home the book she thought would have a record of our Catherine.

Catherine was there all right, but we could not identify her because she was among so many Catherines of the same age, in the same town and county. I felt impressed that I should have a copy of these books, so I asked permission to put the information on family group sheets. Helen agreed to let me copy only until I could find my own relationship. (This was before the copy machine became readily available, so copying was slow, tedious work.)

After spending two years copying these records we had *not* found our Catherine. It was maddening to have all these beautiful records and not be able to submit one sheet because of lack of relationship.

So Helen decided to try to find Catherine for us. Even though she was eighty years old her mind was very keen and she had a tremendous knowledge of the Gulick families. At first she too was unsuccessful. The records were huge. Many families showed ten to fourteen children, plus vital dates and names for many spouses.

After completing the copying of this work, my benefactor found my husband's third great-grandmother, Catherine! One day she presented to me a beautiful deed of Hendrick Gulick naming his daughter Catherine, *the wife of Joseph Kitchen*. From this we were able to make the correct relationship to all the other

Gulick families. Over five hundred names were submitted for ordinance work. The names not submitted were held for further information.

It is difficult to express in words the joy I received when Catherine was correctly identified and all the other names could be submitted. Helen died soon after I copied her records. I am sure she is happy because she was trying to get them in proper order so that when she was gone they could be left to the Genealogical Library in Salt Lake City. Although she did not live to put them there in book form, I am sure her desire has been realized in great measure, in that the greater part of the material is now filed in the library in the form of records of temple work completed.

I wish to bear testimony to the help of our Heavenly Father in obtaining these records. I know I was only an instrument in his hands in bringing forth these names; but for that great privilege I am thankful.

From a Mississippi Postmaster

Jean Anne Bowman

Since I was the first member of my family to join The Church of Jesus Christ of Latter-day Saints, I felt weighed down by the awesome responsibility of finding my ancestors and seeing that temple ordinance work was done for them. I remember that genealogical research at first was very confusing and discouraging to me because I really did not know what to do. This was many years ago, before the modern records we have today were available. But I prayed and continued writing letters and going to the library.

I knew very little about my family. After three years of gathering names I could not identify any one of them as being definitely related to me.

One day as I was working on my records I realized that I was lost. I didn't know what step to take in any of the possible directions. I knelt by my bed and reviewed to my Heavenly Father what I had done so far. I told him that I did not know what to do, that I knew that my great-grandmother, Lucy Eavensen, was ready to have her work done because every time I knelt down to pray I felt her near me. I also felt the presence of her family and knew that they were also ready. But I did not know where the family came from.

I remember that I said: "Heavenly Father, it may be that I'm ignorant, but I have worked hard, and now I have to have thy help. Please help me to know how to find Lucy Eavensen."

As I closed my prayer something like a voice in my head told me to write to a postmaster in a certain city in Mississippi. (At that time I didn't know that postmasters are a suggested reference source. This idea was something new and foreign to me.)

I wrote and mailed the letter to that postmaster, enclosing in it an outline of the information I had and asking him to put the letter in the hands of anyone who might know something about my great-grandmother.

Not many weeks later I received a letter from a man who had received my letter from the postmaster. This man happened to know a lady in another city who was related to my Eavensen people. I wrote to her immediately and she replied that she knew my great-grandmother's name, Lucy, and that my great-grandmother had married William Manning Cason. This woman told me where my great-grandparents came from in Elbert County, Georgia.

This information opened up that whole line! I was able to have the temple work done for my great-grandmother and her parents. Since that time I have been privileged to send in thousands of names on that line and have the ordinance work completed.

I have often wondered what would be the odds on a computer of picking out a postmaster in a city somewhere in the United States and having that postmaster know how to put a letter in the hands of someone who knew your family. I doubt that it is even computable; I feel that only through our Heavenly Father's help could something like this happen.

This was my first spiritual experience while doing genealogical research. Since then I have had many others, every one of them an additional testimony to the truth of the great principle of work for the dead.

What About Mexico?

Lillian M. Archuleta

When I belonged to a small branch of the Church in Los Angeles many years ago, we were taught why genealogy was so important to us. I had a great desire well up within me to do temple work for my family, yet I didn't know how to go about it. I understood that I was to fill out family group sheets and mail them to the Genealogical Society in Utah and that they would do everything that had to be done to complete the temple work for my people. I submitted a few sheets but for some reason I soon put the work aside.

Years passed, and I again developed a great desire to do genealogical research. But I wasn't very organized about it. I didn't know what had been sent in or what work had been done. The information on some of the sheets I had filled in was wrong. I became discouraged again.

Later, when we moved to a new ward, I attended genealogy classes there and began learning the new procedures. But all the class talked about was the United States, England, Sweden, Germany, etc. When I asked, "Well, what about Mexico?" the answer was, "We don't know." I yearned to learn!

There was a sister in our stake who told me to pray to Heavenly Father every time I worked in genealogy. She said,

"Sister Archuleta, kneel and pray and he will guide and direct you." I can testify that he did answer my prayers many times.

I learned how to use the Santa Monica library and I ordered films from Mexico — I don't know how many! In trying to read them I got nauseated, dizzy, disgusted, and my neck hurt; and I didn't understand the writing. I was ordering film from the wrong areas in Mexico. I didn't even know yet from what area my ancestors came. Finally, in desperation, I mailed a letter with a three-dollar money order to a place in Mexico called San Rafael, to the priest of the Catholic church in that town. Supplying all the information I had on my grandfather, I asked for his baptismal certificate. And I prayed, "Heavenly Father, let it be thy will."

About a month later I got a reply which contained my grandfather's baptismal certificate and gave all the details I needed to know, including the names of my paternal and maternal great-great-grandparents. What joy! Since then I've been in contact with that Catholic priest constantly — Reverendo Sr. Obispo. He has in his possession all the books containing the records of my family. When my husband had his vacation in August 1976, we went to Mexico to visit the priest. He personally took us to the town where my grandparents were born. I brought home not only photographs but soil, tree leaves, and rocks from that area and gave some to my uncles and aunts in little jars as presents. They were very pleased; and tears came to their eyes.

Heavenly Father guided my husband and me all through our genealogical trip. Before we left our hotel room we would kneel and pray, and in consequence the Spirit of the Lord was there with us, guiding us and protecting us. We looked through all those precious books. There is one book that dates back to the 1500s.

Every day now I learn more. The advice I give to the young is to start working on your genealogy now. Don't wait until you're older. Your eyes are good and your minds are alert, so begin now!

I still attend genealogy classes. It's my love. I thank Heavenly

Father for being kind and good to me and for helping me find my ancestors. They are always on my mind.

This work is so marvelous, so obviously inspired, that it is a strong testimony to me of the divinity and truth of The Church of Jesus Christ of Latter-day Saints. I thank my Heavenly Father for directing me to his church. I know that Joseph Smith was a mighty Prophet of God and that the President of the Church today is also a prophet, directing and guiding us in the ways of our Heavenly Father.

Inspiration in French Genealogy

Hugh T. Law

Part of my work in the old Research Department of the Genealogical Society of the Church was to do French research for individuals requesting it. (Our library personnel no longer do research for individuals but we assist patrons so that they can do their own research.) Many years ago an elderly lady from Idaho asked me to trace the ancestry of her grandfather, George Panchot, who came to the United States from France in about 1840.

Learning that he and several sons and a stepson had all fought in the Union Army during the Civil War, we obtained copies of their service and pension records. Like the censuses of the time, George's pension application showed only that he was born in France in 1816. It did not give the town or even the region of his birth. It did say, however, that he was married by a Lutheran minister in Buffalo, New York, and that he thought the records of that minister had been lost.

An examination of Catholic records of Buffalo located a marriage record in the early 1840s of a Peter Panchot, son of Christopher and Margaret. A George Panchot was named as a witness, indicating that he was perhaps a brother of Peter.

My patron believed that her grandfather was born in Paris, but research there failed to locate the surname Panchot. A genealogist in Strasbourg, France, wrote me that a Lutheran farmer could only have come from two places in France, Alsace and the area around Montbéliard, an area south of Alsace and near Switzerland.

At that time a Lutheran minister in the Montbéliard area was doing research for another patron of mine. One day I received a large envelope of papers from the minister. He had labeled the various groups of papers by using the backs of spare ballots from his parish, ballots on which members voted for church officers. I filed the papers. Soon after that I analyzed the research for George Panchot. Then I took up again the report from the Lutheran pastor and noticed that on the front side of the ballot paper was named a deacon, George Panchot! He was living in Magny D'Anigon, a small town in the mountainous area near Montbéliard.

Suddenly I received a strong impression: This town was where our George Panchot was born in 1816! I knew it! Nevertheless, I wrote a letter to the town of Magny D'Anigon, asking for extracts of the birth records of George Panchot and his brothers and sisters. I wasn't the least surprised when, a short time later, I received records of George Panchot, born March 29, 1816, son of Christophe and Marguerite, and records of a younger brother named Pierre (Peter).

Research also showed that Pierre did not come to the United States at the same time his parents did, for he was recorded in the conscription records of twenty-year-olds with a statement that his parents, Christophe and Marguerite, had gone to the United States. Marguerite's maiden name was also Panchot, and the Lutheran minister traced this couple's ancestry back as far as the parish records were preserved, supplying family groups at each generation.

This and other impressive experiences in genealogical research have given me a strong testimony that this is a work dear to our Heavenly Father. This experience has strengthened my faith in life after death and in the resurrection as taught in the scriptures.

One Precious Address in Iran

Mike Amini

Not long ago *genealogy* was just another word in my vocabulary. Though I was aware that I should be striving to seek out my ancestors, it was easy to tell myself that I'd do it someday or, better still, I'd let someone else do it for me.

One Sunday I heard the ward genealogy instructor tell of the importance of genealogy. She related some of her beautiful experiences while doing research. She kept saying that we must not leave the work for someone else to do, that we should not start the work "someday" but start it today. She warned us that we would be likely to experience problems and discouragement, but if we were prayerful the answers would come. That meeting was to be a very valuable part of the days that followed in my life.

I am from Iran and am a convert to the Church. For a short time after I came to the United States I kept up correspondence with relatives, but as it became apparent to them that I would not be returning to Iran, many letters I sent were unanswered and communication gradually stopped.

About six months after the meeting in which I heard the genealogy instructor speak, and after watching with interest as my wife and my mother-in-law worked on their genealogy, I began to sense feelings I had not experienced before. I knew within myself

71

that I must do something about my own genealogy. It was rather frightening to realize that I was the only one who could do the research for my family, and I hardly knew where to begin.

Our ward genealogy instructor dropped by our home one evening to encourage our family to get started. I told her that I thought I would have to go to Iran to get the names and dates I needed, because there were no written records kept until recently. She told me what materials I would need to take. She then suggested I start writing letters to see if I could locate any relatives and thus make the trip easier and more fruitful. I appreciated the confidence she had in me, as I lacked confidence or courage at the time.

How could I write letters? I could not remember addresses, and because of moving many times through the years I had long since lost track of the letters I had received from Iran when I first came to America. Several days went by and my frustration grew. Then one day on my way home from work I suddenly recalled the address of my brother. I immediately wrote a letter to him and anxiously waited week after week for a reply.

The beginning of my genealogy work was not to be that easy, however. The letter came back with the notation that there was no such person at that address. Terribly discouraged, I wondered: "What now? Will the trip to Iran do any good if I can't locate any of my family?" Our teacher's counsel, "Don't give up," kept me going. I searched every drawer and every little corner for another address, but found none. *Then I prayed about it*, as I should have done from the beginning. Finally I remembered some old books that I'd had during the first year or two I was in the United States. I began looking through them, knowing they were the last place I had to look. God must have known I was sincere in what I was doing, for I found four old letters, each with a precious address.

But my happiness in finding the letters was followed by doubts and worry. These addresses were twenty years old. Those relatives could have moved or perhaps have even passed away during that time. Still, I knew I had to try. The letters were mailed and the waiting period began again. Nearly three weeks went by and my concern grew. Then it came to me that perhaps I was not doing all I could do; I remembered our instructor saying many times, "Pray about it," and I did pray earnestly during the next few days.

One beautiful day my wife, Alice, called me at work. She was excited to tell me that she had found a letter from Iran. It had been pushed toward the back of the mailbox and apparently had been there unnoticed for several days. The letter was from a very dear uncle whom I had known when I was a boy. I had not written to this uncle because his address was not one of the addresses I'd found. He had accidentally found my letter at the house where my mother had lived and was so excited to know I was alive and well that he copied down my address and wrote to me. He said he hoped I could visit him some day. He also informed me that his son had recently come to America to attend a California university and would undoubtedly be *very* happy to know of his "American" cousin. I was thrilled to learn of the existence of my "first" cousin who was born just three months after my departure from Iran.

After we had completed preliminary arrangements by telephone, my cousin arrived for a very welcome visit with us. At last I had found a link with home! My cousin and I shared many experiences of our homeland and family. He was happy to help with my genealogy and was sure his father would also know many names, dates, and places which would assist me.

My heart is filled with joy because of these special experiences. My prayers have surely been answered. The Lord has prepared the way for me to begin my genealogy work in Iran by not only guiding me to the old books containing the "helpful" letters, but at the same time inspiring my cousin to come to America.

Genealogy is no longer "just another word in my vocabulary." Genealogy is my family here on the earth as well as beyond the veil.

At time of writing, I am scheduled to leave for Iran in four months' time.

IV

Journeys to Ancestral Areas

Question:

I have already reviewed the LDS branch library records of my area of research and still have many unsolved problems. Would there be any point in taking a trip back to the original home of my ancestors?

Aid from a Heater

Jessie Layton Ewing

In the mid-1960s my husband and I were traveling through the central United States checking county courthouse records where our grandparents were known to have lived. On a bitter cold afternoon about a week before Christmas, we drove into the old town of Carlinville, Macoupin County, Illinois. We soon found the only trailer park in town and rented a space for our twenty-one-foot trailer. Unfortunately we were too late to get into the power company office to make a deposit to get electricity. But our trailer had a good propane heater and a gas light, so we felt we could keep warm without our electric blanket.

Imagine our surprise and consternation when the heater, which had always lit instantly with the first match, refused time and time again to light. After wasting a book of matches my husband went to the manager of the trailer park to see where we could get help to repair the heater, as we would freeze without either gas or electricity.

The manager inquired why we were in Carlinville. Learning of our mission, he told my husband about the Moore Cemetery which was located on the farm of my third great-grandfather, Thomas Moore. The manager said that he had framed Thomas Moore's Masonic apron and hung it in the Masonic lodge hall in

77

Carlinville. He gave us the name and address of Helen Moore who had donated the apron. She was a second great-granddaughter-in-law of Thomas Moore who, he said, was a Revolutionary War soldier.

When my husband returned to the trailer, he struck another match, and the heater lit instantly, as it always had before. Never again did it fail to light.

No one will ever convince me that that experience was merely a coincidence; it was the Lord's way of connecting me with my people, none of whom were members of the Church. This was an experience for which I shall be eternally grateful.

We first called upon my new-found cousin, Helen, who gave us quite a bit of family information and sent us to see Ethel Yard, another cousin.

In response to our knock at the door, Mr. Yard met us with outstretched arms, saying, "Come in, come in! We are so glad to see you." I said, "I have never had such a warm reception in all my life. You don't even know who we are." "That makes no difference," came the reply, "we are still happy to have you."

Then his wife, Ethel, came to greet us. She wanted to know where we were from. "Salt Lake City? Are you Mormons?" she asked. I responded in the affirmative. "Then I have another question. Are you converted Mormons or born Mormons?" We couldn't see what difference that made, but I replied: "Both — my husband is a converted Mormon but I'm a born Mormon — which one will you take?" Then we were taken into the living room and seated in front of a cheery fire and a beautiful Christmas tree.

Ethel excused herself but returned in a few minutes with a large box of family records. We spent at least an hour with her going through the records she had been gathering for ten years. She didn't know why she had gathered this material — she just enjoyed doing it. She had records of marriages, births, deaths, family gatherings, property sales, deeds, wills, family letters, and so forth. We asked if we might copy her records, and as there were so many she said we might take them to Salt Lake City with us and mail them back. We said goodnight and returned to our trailer.

In about fifteen minutes there was a rap on the door; outside stood Ethel and Roy Yard, our new-found cousins. We hurriedly invited them in, out of the cold and snow. Ethel handed a large shoe box to us, exclaiming, "Here, I forgot these. I want you to have these too."

My husband and I had never met anyone like these wonderful people. We had met them only a few hours before, and now they were trusting us with all their priceless family records. We knew we would return them all, but how could she know?

We spent a wonderful day at the courthouse gleaning more information on both my Moore and Lewis lines and were invited back to the Yard's home for dinner that evening. Ethel had also invited a houseful of new cousins for us to meet.

While in Carlinville we visited the Moore Cemetery where we found the graves of many of my people. We also saw Grandfather Thomas Moore's Masonic apron. We returned to Carlinville two other summers and found the sites of the homes of my second great-grandparents, Neriah Lewis and Mary Moss, and my great-grandfather, Tarlton Lewis, of the Hauns Mill Massacre fame. His wife was Malinda Gimlin.

Through the help I received from my wonderful new-found cousins in Carlinville and through further research I have been able to do the temple work for a great many of my people. I have also been able to put together missing parts of the family records. I shall always be grateful to the Lord for preventing our heater from lighting that bitter cold December evening in Carlinville so that we might obtain those priceless records.

Ethel Yard died July 25, 1969, and Roy Yard granted me permission to have her temple work done.

79

The Evans Story

Cleo Harman Evans

Part I: (Virginia) Who Needs an Index?

My husband Al had taken a job with the United States government. From the moment we moved back east to Virginia to be close to his work in Washington, D.C., I felt impressed that we should get started on our family records. We knew that Al's ancestor, Robert Evans, was born in Amherst County, Virginia, and here we were, living in the same state.

The first Sunday after we arrived I went to the genealogy class and asked a few questions about where to go to find the Amherst County records. I was told the state library in Richmond, Virginia, would have them. At that time there were no Latter-day Saint branch libraries. In fact, the Church Genealogical Society had not yet made the films available to the public even in Salt Lake City. So to get the courthouse records, a person would have to visit the courthouse or a state library.

It was no easy task to make arrangements for that first trip to Richmond from our home in Northern Virginia. With four little children to take care of, for several years I had procrastinated doing our genealogy. As I was driving the one hundred miles to Richmond, I felt pulled in two directions. I knew I was going to do the Lord's work, but I was also leaving behind my little family to fend for themselves. I was alone and I was frightened. I really prayed that the Lord would guide me and direct me and also protect my family.

In the January 1977 issue of the *Ensign* magazine, Elder Boyd K. Packer's article "Someone Up There Loves You," included the words: "Like Nephi, you will be led by the Spirit, not knowing beforehand the things [you] should do." (1 Nephi 4:6.) That scripture describes my first trip to Richmond perfectly. Brother Packer also told in the same article, "We gathered everything we had together and in the course of a few weeks we were amazed at what we were able to accomplish. The thing that was most impressive, however, was the fact that we began to have experiences that told us somehow that we were being guided, that there were those beyond the veil who were interested in what we were doing. Things began to fall into place."

These were the conditions of my first trip to Richmond. I walked into the library and looked around. It was big, and the room was already filled with people. As I found a table and sat down, I was completely at a loss to know where to begin.

I finally went up to the desk and told the attendant that all I knew was that Robert Evans was supposed to have been born in Amherst, Virginia. She directed me to the bookshelf and also told me of some deed books arranged around the room in alphabetical order by county. The first book I picked up was marriage bonds for Amherst County. I opened the book and there staring at me were the words: *Robert Evans married Martha England (Bond) dated 2 September 1795 – parents William Evans and Elizabeth England.* Only other beginning genealogists will know the joy I felt at that moment. I was so green that I did not realize that there was an index in the back of the book. With the help of the Lord, who needs an index?

The next thing I did was to go over to the other side of the room, where I found two deed books for Amherst County on the shelf. By that time I realized there must be an index, and I now found several entries for William Evans (Robert's father). I began to copy these deeds.

Across the table from me sat a woman I felt to be fascinating. I seemed drawn to her, and I watched her for a few minutes as she industriously worked in some deed books. As I became involved with my Amherst County deeds, I momentarily forgot the woman; and when I looked up, she was gone. I remember how startled I was because she had been there just a moment before. I looked around the room and she had disappeared. Open on the table she had left the book she was working in.

I was impressed to go and look at that book. I got up and walked around the table to see what it was. On the top of the page were the words *Evans to Wheeler*. These words seemed to jump out at me. Again, my heart was filled with joy. I looked to see what book it was. How could this Evans be ours? It was not an Amherst County deed book — it was Albemarle County deeds. I did not understand why I felt so wonderful, because this deed obviously could not be ours, and yet I knew it was. There was no doubt at all. I was so new at doing genealogical research that I did not realize that Amherst County was formed out of Albemarle County. The property of William Evans was in that portion of Albemarle County that became Amherst County.

After that day there was no stopping me. I did work on the Evans line and many others. I had many wonderful experiences and was able to have a lot of temple work done on many different lines. But the Evans story does not end here.

Part II: (Georgia) Satan Thwarted

After Robert Evans and Martha England were married, they moved to the state of Georgia and settled in Elbert County and later Hall County. It was a grandson of Robert Evans named William Romulus Evans, Sr., who joined the Church in 1887 in Dahlonega, Lumpkin County, Georgia. He was one of nine children born to John Maiben Evans, and the only one to join the Church — at a time and place when to do so was to invite persecution. Northern Georgia, with its beautiful mountains, forests, and clear streams had been part of the ancestral home of the Cherokee nation, before that proud and advanced people were forced by the United States Army to make the long and bitter "trail of tears" to the dry plains of Oklahoma (which is a stirring story of its own).

The same spirit which caused the Indians to be forced westward held sway in the Southern States Mission. Converts and investigators were under near-constant persecution; some of the elders had been whipped and actually lynched by mobs.

As grandfather and his first wife were the only ones of the Evans family to join the Church, they also suffered from family displeasure and some persecution from that source as well as from outside. Many of the converts from the southern states were called to leave their homes and colonize the San Luis Valley of Colorado. Grandfather and his young wife joined the exodus west, but the high country and the trials of childbirth took their toll and the young bride passed away shortly after their arrival. The infant daughter lived for only a few weeks before she joined her mother in death. Grandfather married a second time, to Martha Ellen Sego.

Grandfather was able to get only a small portion of the family records as there was still much bitterness toward all Mormons.

In January of 1916, Al's father, William Romulus Evans, Jr., was called to serve a mission in the southern states. He labored some of the time in the homeland of his father. It was amazing how the bitterness and persecution had lingered on after all the time since his father's conversion. He was able to visit some of his cousins and relatives, but for the most part they would have nothing to do with "the Mormons." One of his relatives chased him off the property. He said, "Utah is that way [pointing west] and you can go back there!"

So it was that, after fruitless attempts at trying to obtain family records via mail from relatives, the genealogical research on Grandfather's line came to a standstill for many years.

In the meantime, back in Virginia, we had done about all we could do without taking a trip to Georgia. After hearing all the stories about the bitterness and persecution, we were almost afraid to go. At that time our financial situation would not permit us to go to Georgia. Because of illness and accidents which plagued us during ensuing years, we could never get to the point where we could make the trip. Finally, seven years after that first trip to Richmond, we made a decision to go to Georgia in the summer of 1965 if we had to walk every step of the way!

We informed our families in Utah that we were planning to go and expected some financial help from them. Al kept saying, "Cleo, write to the cousins in Georgia and let them know we are coming"; and I would respond: "They are your relatives. You write." He would reply, "But you're the genealogist." And so it went. I never could bring myself to write to them; so we started off on our trip without letting anyone know we were coming.

We rented a travel trailer and excitedly started on our journey. Our trip nearly ended before it began. We had only gotten a short way down the road, towing our trailer, when an older car shot out from a stop sign without stopping and nearly forced us off the road. The same car was ahead of us on the approach to the freeway, driving as if Satan himself were at the wheel. As he shot onto the interstate highway ahead of us, Al slowed down, wishing to keep well behind him. That decision was indeed fortunate for us, because the hood of his car flew off, shot up over his car, and bounced down the road toward us. We swerved off to the shoulder of the road and the hood bounced on down the road. Had we not swerved it would have hit us. At that point we began to wonder if we were doing the right thing. Was this what was in store for us?

The balance of our trip through North and South Carolina was uneventful. We were able to do related research in Raleigh,

North Carolina, and Columbia, South Carolina. Then into Georgia we went, with some foreboding.

Since many of the Evans descendants lived in Gainesville, Georgia, we planned to camp near there. Prior to setting up our tent trailer, we stopped to do some laundry and make further plans. My husband asked me again if I had written to the relatives to let them know we were coming. "No," I said, "I just couldn't make myself do it." *We* decided, since they were his relatives, that *he* should call them on the phone. It was Saturday afternoon and it was our desire to meet some of them the following day. He made two calls but no one seemed to be home. The third call went through, and a lady's voice said, "Hello."

"Hi," Al said. "You don't know me, but we are related. My name is Al Evans. My wife and I and our son David are camping out on Lake Sydney Lanier. We would really like to come and see you tomorrow and talk to you about our great-great-grandfather, John Maiben Evans."

"Well, I don't know. I'm not very well," the voice replied.

"We don't want to impose on you at all. We just want to meet you."

"Well, I guess it will be all right."

So it was arranged — we would meet at ten the next morning. When we were through at the laundromat we drove around the countryside of Al's grandfather's birth. It was beautiful, and we cannot express in words the way we felt. We thanked the Lord that we had made it and we felt sure that the purpose of our trip was going to be realized.

That evening we cooked dinner by the beautiful lake and really had an enjoyable time together. When it was turning dusk, we decided to put the camp in order and prepare to go to bed. My husband was standing on a slope. Suddenly I heard a cry and turned to see him down on the ground in agony. A small pebble under his foot had rolled, throwing him off balance. Twice before

85

he had broken his right kneecap, and it had been removed. From all appearances, he had re-injured his knee joint. It had immediately swollen as big as a basketball.

I ran to the next camp for help, and two men came and helped him into our car. As I was driving to the nearest hospital, we were both weeping. Al said, "Why — why would the Lord allow this to happen, after all we have been through, all the prayers and preparation?" All I could say was: "I don't know. I don't understand."

A few hours later we learned the bitter truth. The doctors said that he would not be able to camp for some time and would have to be in a cast for six weeks. They wanted to admit him to the hospital. He refused both the hospital bed and the cast, pleading with the doctors that he could not travel back home with a cast on his leg. The doctor taped his leg and gave us a prescription for pain medication.

After getting Al to bed in a motel, our son Dave and I went looking for an all-night drugstore to get some crutches. For the rest of the night in the motel which we were now forced to rent, we finally went to sleep with bitter tears because it was obvious that all our plans were in disarray. Our finances would not allow us to stay in motels, and Al's leg would not allow us to camp. Worse still, the walking requirements to do research appeared beyond Al's capabilities.

The next morning Dave and I knelt by Al's bed and prayed that the way would be opened for us to get the genealogical information and that hearts would be softened to receive us. As we arose, we knew that we would be successful.

We kept our ten o'clock appointment. As we got out of the car at the appointed place, the relatives came out to greet us with smiling faces and outstretched hands. When they heard what had happened to us the night before, their hearts literally melted. From that point on they could not do enough for us. They made us cancel our motel reservation, and the Sheffields of Flowery

Branch and Annabelle Johnson of Gainesville adopted us. They called a lot of relatives and made arrangements to take us to cemeteries, courthouses, etc. Family records were generously handed over to us. We were grateful beyond our ability to express.

No one seemed to know where John Maiben Evans was buried. And even though we went through many cemeteries we could not find his grave. It was in connection with this that what is perhaps the most unusual occurrence happened. On the same Saturday that we were driving into Georgia, another cousin, Jett Allison, was driving past the Wahoo Church cemetery. Neither she nor anyone else knew we were there or even that we were coming. As she looked at the cemetery, she wondered what condition her grandfather's and grandmother's graves were in. She pulled over and walked through the cemetery. It was in terrible condition. The graves were all overgrown with weeds. She could not even find the grave of John Maiben Evans.

Exasperated, Jett left immediately and hired a boy. Together they worked all that Saturday, cleaning out the weeds. That was how she found Grandmother and Grandfather Evans's gravestones, which had fallen down and were broken in several pieces. We ourselves probably *never* would have found them.

It was on Monday that we went to see Jett. When we asked her if she knew where Grandfather's grave was, she told us what she had done the Saturday before. There was no doubt in our minds that we were being guided, that we were being helped by those beyond the veil on our genealogy trip to Georgia!

Part III: (North Carolina) Delayed Significance

I was doing genealogical research on one of my husband's lines (Crowder) in the Rutherford County, North Carolina, records, when I read that there was a Zions Baptist Church cemetery in the county. I wrote a letter to the minister of that church asking for information on what records they had. I did not tell him which family name I was interested in, only that we would be traveling down that way soon and were wondering what might be available for us to look at.

The minister surmised that, because my name was Cleo Evans, I was doing research on the Evans line. He went to a lot of work collecting family data on a man by the name of David Evans who had settled in the county in the 1700s. He made personal visits to descendants of this man. He also copied records from the church records.

When I received the "thick" pack from this good Christian minister I was sick at heart, for our Evanses never lived in the state of North Carolina, let alone in that county. I wondered what I could do with all that material that he had spent so much time preparing.

A week later a sister in my ward asked me if I would please help her with her genealogy. As I sat down and began to look over her records, I could not believe what I saw. Her great-grandfather was the David Evans of Rutherford County, North Carolina! Can you imagine her surprise when I was able to hand her all that material on her ancestors! Tears of joy streamed down her face and mine.

There never was a truer statement made than, "God moves in a mysterious way, his wonders to perform." It is so marvelous to be in a small way a participant in and a witness of the wonders performed in gathering family data in the last days.

His Life's Work — My Kikapoo People

Harlan Reed

As I analyze our 1976 trip to Texas and Oklahoma, I can see the hand of the Lord in our disappointments as well as our joys.

I always have had a love for airplanes, and when an air museum in Paris, Texas, offered a pilot's course in their vintage airplane, I fell for it. My wife, Jan, and I planned for a month-long experience in flying, with a two- or three-day side trip to Oklahoma to do some genealogical research, since my father's tribe has its headquarters in Shawnee.

After getting up the courage to go, saving money, and anxiously waiting, we were finally on our way. It was a long drive from Seattle to Paris, Texas, but the excitement kept us going. Upon arrival, however, everything suddenly changed when my flying plans fell through. "My" plane had been crash-landed just a week before. What a disappointment! I remember that I had asked the Lord if the trip was at all feasible and received a wonderful feeling about it. And now this had happened! Why had we come all this way, some fifteen hundred miles, only to find we had made a mistake?

Discouraged, Jan and I drove north across the Texas-Oklahoma border and followed the Indian Nation Turnpike. As we drove through the solid-green forest, I kept thinking about my prayer. I'd had such a good feeling about the trip. What had happened?

We arrived in Shawnee two days before the American Bicentennial weekend. We were starting our genealogical research literally from scratch, with only our prayers to guide us. We began by looking through the telephone book for my relatives. I had visited Shawnee as a child and could still remember a few of my aunts and uncles. As we visited each one, we were referred to many other relatives I'd never heard of who also lived in or near Shawnee. I felt happy to see them after so many years of separation from the family, but I could sense a bit of antagonism and resentment from them because of the work we were doing. A few relatives wouldn't see us because of a long-standing family feud over land and inheritance rights.

Nevertheless, we learned many things about my father's people. One thing we discovered was their belief that one should never mention the name of a person who has died. The burials are secret and the graves are unmarked. The Kikapoo people have no written language, and consequently records are generally unobtainable. All of these details made us wonder if we would find anything. We still felt that the Lord was with us, though, and that gave us strength to keep on looking.

Next we went to the Shawnee Bureau of Indian Affairs (BIA) office, where we found a gold mine of Mexican Kikapoo names, dates, and relationships dating back to the late 1800s. The sparkle in my eyes must have been visible as we asked the office attendant question after question. The office had stacks of neatly filed cards with all the information we needed, not only for my family but for the whole tribe. Jan and I worked feverishly but couldn't get all the information down before closing time. Because it was a special holiday weekend, we had to wait four days before we could begin our research again.

The days seemed like an eternity, but with the help of the small Shawnee ward we had a very spiritual Sunday and were ready for more record-searching when Tuesday came.

90

On Tuesday afternoon we finally completed copying the land records and interviewing family members. Before leaving for home we made one last stop on Wednesday at the archives of the Oklahoma Historical Society. The society had a special library on all the Indian tribes in Oklahoma. We found various documents on my father's tribe, including some Indian census and land allotment records.

A librarian helped us as we searched through the stacks of historical information. She showed us many sources and then mentioned a man named Mr. Slack, a retired BIA man, who had done extensive research on the Mexican Kikapoo Tribe. She showed us the index to his work on the tribe. It seemed to be quite thorough, since my name was listed and I had never lived in or around the tribe. We discovered that there were six volumes of his work but that the library didn't have them. We decided to call him and make an appointment to see him personally.

As we talked on the telephone I began to appreciate Mr. Slack. He said he would be glad to show us the volumes if we would pick them up at the BIA office. This we couldn't understand; no one in the BIA office had mentioned the records when we were there before. We drove the fifty miles back to Shawnee and to the BIA office, where we obtained the volumes and the index after some discussion and another telephone call to Mr. Slack. We then went to see him.

As we talked, the story of the records became clear. It had taken him twenty-six years to compile the volumes to aid him in his BIA work. During those twenty-six years he became a trusted friend of the Indians in his area, so much so that he was able to gain an intimate knowledge of their family relationships and their customs. The six volumes are proof of the confidence they must have had in him. We asked Mr. Slack if we could have the volumes microfilmed at the Genealogical Library in Salt Lake City. He was overjoyed that someone else thought them of value and told us to take the records with us and return them when it was convenient.

91

Needless to say, we left Oklahoma feeling that we had really accomplished a great deal. We came away with the knowledge that we truly can do the impossible with the Lord guiding us. We believe sincerely that the Lord inspired Mr. Slack to love my father's people and that similarly the Lord guided us and protected us on our trip.

I know that if we seek to do the will of the Lord a way will be made for us to accomplish it. I believe that genealogy is a great work.

An Encounter in England

Deloris A. Hill

Time seemed to be passing rapidly. I was busily engaged in teaching an English genealogical research class and at the same time making preparations for a field trip to England. As I planned my itinerary, it occurred to me that Sylvia Thatcher, one of the sisters in my class, had a difficult research problem in the Huntington-Northampton area, one place I had planned to include in my work. Knowing the scarcity of records available in the United States on that area, I felt compelled to call Sister Thatcher and ask if she would be interested in my trying to find some data on her family while I was in England. She was delighted at the idea and proposed a trade. She would paint an oil portrait of my daughter in exchange for the work I would do for her. It was agreed.

July found me at the Huntington record office. The archivist graciously assisted me in obtaining the records I requested, and I was soon deeply engrossed in study and extraction. An hour or so later the office door opened and a tall man of about thirty years of age came in and began working at a nearby table. Some time later I was startled to hear a voice say, "Are you one of the people involved in the population survey?" Since we were the only two people in the office he was obviously directing his inquiry to me.

93

I looked up and explained that I was from the United States and was doing some research in the bishop's transcripts of Great Giddings for a friend of mine. The man asked what name I was interested in. I replied, "Southwell." He immediately corrected my American pronounciation of the name to "Suthell," and then said, "That wouldn't be the Southwell that married the Wade, would it?"

I was so amazed that I thought my ears had deceived me. What would a complete stranger know of the same family I had come thousands of miles to seek out? Upon regaining my composure I answered: "Why, yes it is. Do you know of the family?"

The man introduced himself. I was surprised to learn that he was a parish minister and was historically interested in the families of the area. He said: "I have made a study of families in a nine-parish area, including Great and Little Giddings and their adjoining parishes. I have made a surname card file of these findings, and I know I have data on the family you are working on. Would you like a copy of what I have?"

I explained to him that I would only be in Huntington until four o'clock that afternoon, when I had to catch a bus for the next leg of my journey, and that I planned to be in Northampton the next morning. We exchanged addresses, and he promised to mail the data to me. He then promptly left, as he was on his way to attend to business matters elsewhere.

A couple of hours later, once again deeply engrossed in study, I was startled to hear the archivist say, "Mrs. Hill, you are wanted on the telephone." With quaking knees and great apprehension, fearing that something had happened to my loved ones back in the states, I went to the phone. I was surprised to hear the voice of the reverend. He said: "After conversing with you and learning you were leaving for Northamptonshire this afternoon, I decided to return home and check my records. Here are a few items from the Southwell file I thought you should have which might aid in your research in Northampton."

The information was indeed valuable, and as I proceeded with my research the next day in Northampton, I felt greatly blessed to find much information pertaining to the ancestral Southwell families.

Thinking back on this experience, I am thoroughly convinced that the assistance of the Almighty was present. I asked myself these questions:

1. Why was it that this gentleman would appear on the *only* day I would be in Huntington?

2. What compelled him to speak to me and inquire as to my purpose there?

3. Why should he so immediately recall the family of interest to me?

4. What compelled him to return home, before proceeding to his business affairs, to search his file for information that was extremely important to me in my searches in Northamptonshire?

As a result of this experience, it was possible to complete the family record of Sister Thatcher's great-grandparents, as well as to extend the Southwell pedigree several generations.

I will never forget this almost unbelievable experience. I am sure Sister Thatcher's prayers were answered through me in behalf of her Southwell ancestors.

This is only one of several faith-promoting and testimony-building experiences that have happened during the course of my genealogical activities. Whether working on my own lines, on my husband's lines, or even on the lines of others, many instances have occurred that I feel can only be explained through help from our Heavenly Father.

Concern for the "Kakocho"

Shigeki Ushio

When Sono Ushio, a young bride of two months, landed in San Francisco in 1913 and proceeded inland with her husband, Matajiu (Fujiwara) Ushio, she was starry-eyed with excitement and expectation and hope for a future in the state of Utah. Only one gnawing concern marred her happiness. She was the last of her family line, and her responsibility to her family name and her ancestral dead weighed heavily on her pretty head.

Sono was born on February 10, 1890, to a merchant family whose more distant past included battles and wars, fire and massacres, and narrow escapes from utter extinction in feudal Japan.

The early life of Sono in Onomichi City, Hiroshima, a seaport city on the shores of the Beautiful Inland Sea in southern Japan, was quite pleasant. She was educated in the best schools and was taught all of the skills that a proper young girl needed to know.

Later, however, tragedy and unhappiness struck in rapid succession. First her only sister died, then her only brother died of a lingering illness without leaving any heirs. Sono's father, Rinhichi Ushio, had left the management of the family business in the hands of a brother-in-law and gone abroad to study art in France and in the United States. After many years of study he

96

returned to Japan, only to contract a fatal illness and die before ever reaching his home and family. The brokenhearted wife and mother followed her husband in death, and Sono was left all alone. Her family's business had been squandered by bad management, so Sono went to live with her aunt.

As was the custom in Japan, where great significance was placed on the family and on the continuity of the family name, a marriage was arranged for Sono with a young man from the Fujiwara family who agreed to assume and to perpetuate the Ushio name. Matajiu Fujiwara had previously emigrated to and lived in America, so he took his new bride and his new name (Matajiu Frank *Ushio*) back to America in the quest for the Great American Dream. Two boys and a girl blessed their union, and for half a century the Ushio family worked hard to achieve a measure of success in their new home. Throughout these years Sono Ushio was continually concerned with her responsibility to the Ushio family name, and she repeatedly sent money and letters to Japan asking for the family records that she knew were in existence. Repeatedly the messages came back that the records were either lost or destroyed or otherwise nonexistent.

The Ushio family joined The Church of Jesus Christ of Latter-day Saints, Grandmother Sono being baptized in 1953. In 1965 a grandson, David Ushio, was called on a mission to Japan. At the conclusion of the mission, David and his parents, Shigeki and Momoko Ushio, visited their relatives in Japan. There in the dust and debris of fifty years' accumulation behind a "butsudan" in Grandmother Sono's former home, the Ushio family records were found! They were inscribed on very old parchments which were folded accordion-like into a compact packet. The records of birth, deaths, and marriages went back for eight or more generations.

In Japan the Ushios made arrangements at the Buddhist Temple for perpetual care and attention for the physical remains of the family burial plots and for a simple traditional religious ceremony for the departed. The records, which were called the

97

"Kakocho," became the basis for extensive temple work for the dead in the Salt Lake Temple. A lifetime of concern and a sense of responsibility for the family name and for the ancestral dead for Sono Ushio was finally satisfied.

White Horse on the Barn Doors

Coby Van Mastright

Almost immediately after our baptism, my husband Wim and I started working on our genealogies. We were both born in Holland. In order to get a good start we wrote to many of our older relatives and asked for information, which in all cases was given to us.

In 1969 I had the opportunity to go from Turkey, where we were then living, to Holland for six weeks, with the express purpose of doing some firsthand genealogical research. While visiting a favorite aunt, I started talking about the family, and my aunt remembered things that she had not thought of for many years. She mentioned visiting her grandfather when she was a little girl in the 1890s and remembered that he had painted a life-size white horse on his barn doors.

This horse intrigued me very much, and for some reason I felt sure that it was still there. Why I should be so sure some seventy years later I do not know; for when I think about it, it seems a bit farfetched to expect an outdoor painting to survive that long! I took my aunt along in the car, however, and we set out to find my great-grandfather's farmhouse. Since my aunt didn't remember exactly where it used to be (it was all so long ago), we did not find it.

99

The following year my husband went to Europe, mostly to Paris, London and Stockholm, on a business trip, and I again went to Holland. When he came to pick me up for our return flight home, he said that he wanted to see the area from which my family came. I love that beautiful area. We rented a car and enjoyed roaming around for the short time we had before departure. We kept alert for any horses painted on any barn doors, but there were none. Then, while we were driving over a very narrow country lane which was just wide enough for our car, at the end of a long driveway I saw a white horse painted on a barn door! We were very excited, but as we did not have any time to spare, Wim just took a few pictures and off we went to the airport.

In 1971 we were in Holland again before returning from Turkey to the United States. The first thing we did was to pick up my aunt and drive back to the farmhouse (which, sure enough, was the one formerly owned by her grandfather).

When we arrived I rang the doorbell and told the old farmer who answered the door that we thought his farm had once belonged to my great-grandfather. At first he seemed a bit suspicious, but then he asked my great-grandfather's name, which I said was Jan van Vliet. At this his face lit up, and we were all invited inside the house. The reason for his pleasure was a surprise to us all. He said that my great-grandfather had written and published a few books and that he had copies of them. He said that he had read and re-read them many times. Naturally we wanted to buy the books from him, but he would not sell them. He gave us some addresses of people in the area whom he thought might have some of the books also.

We chased around the countryside for the whole day in search of the books. Just as we were becoming discouraged about finding anything at all, we came to the house of a minister of the Dutch Reformed Church who collected and sold books from old estates. He knew immediately what we had in mind and was sure that he had some of my great-grandfather's books for us. Unfortunately, it was almost Saturday evening and the minister still had to write his sermon for the following day. Not only that, but his book collection was a bit disorganized and he did not know exactly where the books were. Hoping for the best, we left our address with him.

Quite a while after this visit I received in the mail a copy of a very old book entitled *Letters, Meditations and Spiritual Thoughts* by Jan van Vliet. In it I found some very valuable genealogical information! It also contained much other material which helped me to really get to know this great-grandfather. A few more copies of this same book have shown up and are now with some other members of the family, but we have not been able to locate any of his other books as yet.

The white horse is still on the barn door because each of the farmers who lived there after Jan van Vliet valued the painting enough to touch it up every spring; it looks as if it was painted not too long ago. We are so grateful that the painting was preserved.

For a birthday Wim gave me two enlarged and framed pictures which he had taken of the farm. With their matte finish they are so beautifully done that they almost look like paintings. They always have a special spot in our house and have become real conversation pieces. The white horse on the barn doors is symbolic to us and our children of the quaint traditions, the family history, and the eternal commitments of our family. The painting and our experience in finding it added zest to the important work of submitting our unified family records for temple ordinance work. We have a testimony of that great work.

V

Valuable Records Preserved

Question:

I left all my genealogical records on a bus and never recovered them. Most are replaceable, but it surely will be a lot of hard work replacing them. I've heard of experiences in which valuable records have been miraculously preserved. I wonder if there's any hope for mine.

Miracle in Microfilming

Molimau Tupa'i

On April 9, 1971, The Church of Jesus Christ of Latter-day Saints sent me to the South Pacific to microfilm vital records in the government offices of the various islands. My first stop was Fiji. When I started filming, the Registrar General gave me a key to the office so that I could start work as early as I wanted and stay as late as I wanted.

While my wife and I were in Fiji, in the month of September 1971, the island was hit with a terrible storm, "Hurricane Bebe," which lasted almost a full week. It was an unforgettable experience. At night the wind blew unceasingly. The trees, roof tops, and rocks were unable to withstand such hurricane power.

The government ordered every employee to go home and protect his family as much as possible from the storm. I went to our temporary lodging and found my wife very frightened. We prepared for the storm as best we could.

The day after the hurricane I went down to the office to check on my equipment. On the ground level of that government building there is a drop of about four inches inside the doors and all the doors open inward. There is no carpet in any of the offices on the ground level of the building; the flooring is all tile. As I opened the door, the sound and feel of water being pushed told me the office was flooded. When I heard that sound I rushed to my office with the thought that the books, films and maps I had left on the floor would all be ruined. There was no doubt in my mind that they would be.

As I ran to my little corner, I noticed that everything along the way was wet and severely damaged. But to my surprise I found that in the area containing my books, films, etc., the water was actually flowing away from my material on the floor. None of it had been touched by water. Everything on the table too, where the camera was set up, was all right; nothing was damaged. To me it was a miracle.

By this time other people were starting to come in. Their faces lit up when they saw what had happened, the miracle they were witnessing in my little corner. The Registrar General could scarcely believe it. "Why?" he said. "The floor is as level as you can possibly get it. There is no way that water can flow away like that."

We spent most of the morning cleaning up. I started to film that same afternoon, and the crowd piled into my little corner asking me why I had electricity and they did not.

I too was puzzled. On Thursday and Friday of that same week, I was the only one in the building that had electricity. The outlet into which my equipment was plugged was not any different from any other outlet in the building. Yet I was the only one out of the whole building that had electric power to work with.

The rest of the ground-level floor of the building was a complete mess. A cleaning crew came in, and all regular work was stopped there for days while they cleaned up. But my work proceeded normally in my undamaged corner.

I enjoyed this spiritual experience. It helped me to know how important genealogy is. Others who witnessed this were also impressed that microfilming these records is the will of God. It also proved to me that nothing can frustrate the Lord's plans for his kingdom, but that his work must go on.

I bear a firm testimony that this really happened as I have described it.

(This experience was witnessed by the following persons, who signed a document to that effect:

Molimau Tupa'i
Tamara Tupa'i
Alexander Lobendahl
Penaia Uluibua
Mr. Singth Khan — Fiji Government Registrar General)

A Burning Testimony

Roger Collier

It had been only a few months since our grandmother had come to live with us, along with her treadle sewing machines, bottled fruit, cloth scraps for quilting, and a collection of old documents and genealogy. At the time we had lived in our ward for only about a year and were still in the process of learning names and making friends. The ward was typical of wards throughout the Church, filled with friendly people who were busy with the hustle and bustle of meetings and other activities.

Our family has an abundance of boys; seven to be exact. The oldest is Jay, then myself, then Derek, Scot, Kim, Trent, and John. Jay was on a mission in the Gulf States at the time. I had just turned nineteen and was indecisive about going on a mission. My parents gave me a lot of encouragement, but I had to make up my own mind.

The little white house we lived in was filled to the brim with family. We even squeezed in a goldfish who entertained us by dancing back and forth in his bowl when we set it in front of the television set. It was a cozy home and we learned what together-ness really means. With Jay on a mission and Grammy (the name we've always called my mother's mother) living with us, we had nine all together. We were in the process of expanding the little house by finishing a large full basement and adding a couple of rooms to the west side. This expansion would give us plenty of room, but it wasn't finished yet. We had to make do by most of us boys sleeping on bunk beds in the same room.

One night when we were sound asleep Mom and Dad came through the house with urgency in their voices, telling us: "Go outside. The house is on fire!" I remember awakening in a smoky room, jumping off of the top bunk, grabbing my quilt and running outside. I thought everyone was safe outside, but suddenly we realized that Grammy hadn't come out yet. Without a second thought, my father rushed back into the house. By this time the fire had grown into an uncontrollable blaze, roaring out from underneath and up the side of the house.

My father said that the minute he went through the door he couldn't breathe. Holding his breath, he felt his way to Grammy's room. There he saw a flashlight shining about through the smoke. Grammy was gathering her genealogical and other important papers together in a small suitcase. Dad reached for the flashlight, caught hold of Grammy's hand, turned and headed out. Grammy managed to stay on her feet, but she dropped the suitcase. Leading Grammy, Dad hurriedly felt his way along, and at one point he lost his direction. Fire was beginning to climb up the inside of the walls. The smoke was too thick to see through, the air too smoke-filled to breathe. While trying to find a way out, Dad found a window, and he was ready to break it and throw Grammy out to safety when he heard Scot's voice yelling, "This is the way." Soon they were outside in the fresh air.

We stood back and watched the fire rapidly devour everything we owned. A kind family across the street took us in and put clothes on our backs. Sirens heralded the arrival of the fire engines, and the streets quickly filled with people and excitement. But there was nothing we could do to save our home. With a helpless feeling we got into the car and drove away. The rest of that night we spent at Grandma Collier's home.

A beautiful spring day followed the dawn, and the singing of the birds chased away all our bad dreams. Things seemed to be much brighter and more hopeful. We decided to drive back home and see what had been saved. As we neared our street, we all leaned forward to see what was left, and as we turned the corner we found only a black hole in the ground. We were shocked as a nightmare became a reality. This black hole of ours was a pretty sad-looking sight, and it brought an air of depression over all of us. But as I looked into the charred rubble, I realized something: we were all safe; none of us was down there mixed with the debris. Suddenly I felt very blessed and protected; nothing else mattered, for we had each other. Soon everyone felt the same way.

The next week or so went by quickly, during which time we stayed with our Uncle Don and his family. Bishop Crapo ordered some emergency clothing for us, and we also received some work shoes and clothes. Some of the things came from the same bishops storehouse where I remember I had put in welfare hours and had wondered who would be using the goods produced there. At Uncle Don's we watched television and listened to news bulletin after news bulletin about the fire. We still couldn't believe that the commentators were talking about us. The news reported that the fire was so hot that the water from the water hoses had turned to steam before reaching the blaze, which hampered fire-fighting efforts. The heat had blistered the paint on cars twenty feet away and melted the tail lights of a trailer parked with them.

Bishop Crapo talked to my parents about rebuilding, and he felt that if we did we would get some volunteer help. After looking at several homes and talking it over, my parents decided to rebuild. Brother Holt, a counselor in the bishopric, took the assignment of supervising the building. Someone suggested that we start the fire again to finish burning the debris, but first we wanted to see if there was anything worth salvaging. We spent a few days going through the remains of our belongings. We found the rubber soles of our boots and shoes, the twisted metal that once was our bunk beds, and a lot of old burned rags. I was looking for my new watch and remembered laying it on the piano when I went to bed that eventful night. But now all I could find of the piano was a large metal frame, burned and rusted, though all the strings were still strung. I gave up looking for my watch. The doorway that entered the bathroom upstairs was still standing, only now it was in the basement.

We were all black and smelled of smoke, but we found some interesting things, such as the remains of Kim's accordion, my mother's burned wallet still holding ten dollars, and a piece of the guitar I had once cherished so dearly. More interesting things turned up; someone found the birthday present my aunt had given me, a missionary triple combination still in its cellophane wrapper.

Grammy would often ask if we had found anything of the suitcase containing her genealogical records. We hadn't, and we didn't have much hope of finding it. But we were surprised to uncover many photographs. Some were pictures of us as babies and as young children; some were of our parents as young children. One was of Mom and Dad when they were engaged; one was of Grammy as a young girl with a boyfriend. All of these pictures were lying around loose, yet many of the albums had been burned. I wondered why these pictures had survived when a piano had not.

While cleaning up in preparation for digging a new basement, Brother Holt stumbled across something. It was small, burned and battered and resembled a suitcase. He took it over to the house we were renting and there he, my mother and Grammy opened it. To their astonishment they found in it the genealogical records and other documents Grammy had been so worried about. The suitcase was badly burned, but the contents were safe.

God has frequently shown forth his hand in miracles which increase our testimony and our faith in him. One such miracle was

111

the preserving of the genealogical papers, the patriarchal blessing and the citizenship papers Grammy had been praying about. (Grammy and my mother were converts to the Church in Canada and later came to America and became citizens.) Another was the miracle of giving exhibited by Brother Holt in particular as he spent many long hours on the new house, but also by other people in our ward and stake who greatly helped out with a variety of skills and many of whom we had never met before.

As time passed, all these events had their effect on my heart. I pondered my blessings and the blessings of my family. As I knelt in prayer, I asked God how I could show my gratitude for all his blessings. He answered me clearly and quietly, "Go on a mission." I knew it was right, so I went. My mission to Southern California was a testimony-sharing and testimony-building experience. I referred to our fire several times in talks and shared these miracles with others.

I know that God lives, for I have seen him pour blessings into the lives of his people. While he may allow us to experience hardship and trials, as he did my family, if we keep our attitudes right we will grow through them. I have learned that if we open our eyes we will see miracles going on all around us.

Grandma's Trunk

Phyllis Horner

From my recollections as a child, I know that my grandmother, Mercy H. Parker, was a conscientious genealogical worker. She became a life member of the Genealogical Society of Utah. Before she passed away at the age of eighty-six, she gave my mother (her eldest daughter) a small, dark red, tin trunk containing her genealogical records. This included not only records on her own family line but on her husband's, on some of my father's, and on other family lines touching hers.

Grandma had put many precious hours of her life into collecting and assembling these records. She asked my mother to pass on the trunk and its contents to my young brother when the time seemed right, so that he would then become the family representative. In the meantime my father continued the work.

After my father's death my mother became ill and went to stay with her younger sister and brother-in-law in Grandma's old home. At this time I was married and the mother of six children. My brother had already begun helping Mother gather more information to add to the contents of the trunk. When Mother eventually passed away, however, I found no trace of the trunk among her belongings. I mentioned the matter to my brother; he said it was at my aunt's home. Apparently all was well.

At the time of my aunt's passing, my brother had not collected the trunk, so he gave me permission to ask my uncle if I could have it. My uncle agreed, but he said that the trunk was not in the house but down in the old tumbledown shed at the bottom of the yard.

My uncle let me search, but I could find no sign of the trunk either in the shed or in the house. I could not believe that the records were completely lost and that all the work which had gone into compiling the records in that trunk was in vain. I knew my aunt would have kept them and felt that my uncle would not have burned the records or discarded the trunk without first looking inside, in which case he would have realized the value of the contents.

In due course my uncle became ill and died, leaving the house to his nephews Noel and David. I asked permission to search once more for the trunk before they sold the property. Noel said that I could go through my grandmother's things while he and his wife were preparing the home for sale.

I had hunted high and low and it was time to leave, but I had not found the trunk. I stood still in the passageway, and as I thought of my grandmother I quietly but desperately uttered the words, "Lord, if it's still here somewhere, please don't let me leave without it."

Noel walked into the passageway just as I finished my silent prayer. Just then we heard bumping noises coming from under the house.

The home was built so low to the ground that there was barely enough room between floor and ground for a small child to wriggle around snake-wise. As Noel and I went to investigate we found that the little entrance door to the crawl space was open. Children's excited voices now mingled with thumps and dragging sounds. The very irate father demanded that the children come out at once. As they emerged, they dragged out what they declared to be a treasure chest. The box was covered with an inch-thick coating of dirt and certainly resembled a small treasure chest. Indeed it was a treasure chest, for when we opened it the inside was shiny, dark red tin; and its contents, Grandmother's genealogical records, were clean and in perfect order. Grandmother's efforts had not been in vain.

Twice Rescued

Jared Suess

My mother was instrumental in converting my father to the Church in 1935. As sweethearts, during one of their evening strolls in the beautiful forest near Altstetten, Switzerland, she told him about Joseph Smith, and he was very impressed with the story. They continued dating, but he was quite difficult to convert. He wanted to know everything about the Church before he joined — all the doctrine, the history, and so on.

My mother then invited Carl Ringger, an influential businessman and a Church leader in the Zurich Branch in Switzerland, to talk to my father. (Brother Ringger later became the first patriarch in the Switzerland Zurich Stake.) It took my father about a year until he was converted, and he was baptized at about the time I was born.

My parents were always keenly interested in genealogical research. My mother's mother had hired Julius Billeter, a famed Swiss researcher and a member of the Church, to research her lines. When my father joined the Church, he also was instrumental in getting many lines searched. At that time it was difficult for a layman to get access to the actual records, so the Saints had the very capable Brother Julius Billeter search the lines for them.

My parents were always concerned about temple work, about going to the temple themselves. At that time the Swiss Temple had not been built, so they decided to come to America at the end of World War II. My parents prepared for this long journey just after the war, when travel was still quite difficult. My parents, sisters, and I traveled by train through France and then through Belgium. The train stopped at the border in Luxembourg around midnight and all persons aboard had to have their personal belongings inspected. For some reason some of our belongings were taken off the train and were not put back on. My father suddenly had an inspiration that he ought to go outside and just check to see if everything was all right, even though the train was ready to pull out in about a minute. Outside he found our suitcase which contained all of our genealogical records — thousands and thousands of names — left near the railroad tracks. If he hadn't had this inspiration to go out and check, these records would have been lost. To our family this is a faith-promoting incident and we are grateful that my father had the insight and inspiration to go out and check. This was the first narrow escape our records had.

A short time after my family had come to the United States a man came to our home and wanted to look at our records. My parents let him borrow one of the large Julius Billeter books. Each book contained some three thousand to six thousand names. My parents had been copying information from these books onto family group sheets. The man did *not* return the book.

Many years passed, I had married, and my wife and I were busy in the Church. In the year 1965 I was approaching my graduation from the University of Utah, and since I carried a full academic load it was somewhat of a struggle to finish school. One day I came home at noon quite discouraged because I was trying to earn good grades and was deluged with work to do and papers to prepare. It seemed impossible.

My wife was working, but she felt impressed to come home for lunch that day. She was pleasantly surprised to see me home from my morning classes. I did a bit of grumbling about my studies and

117

so forth, and my wife suggested that I quit worrying because everything would be all right. She said, "Why don't you come back with me and I'll drop you off at the Genealogical Library where you can spend the afternoon?"

I wasn't enthusiastic about this suggestion, but she thought it would do me some good. She knew that I had once had some interest in genealogy, especially during the time when, as a youngster, I had emigrated with my family from Switzerland to the United States. Then my interest declined until it disappeared. After I got married the bishopric asked me to teach the Sunday School genealogy class, along with serving as assistant ward clerk. I didn't really want to teach this class but nevertheless agreed because the bishop thought it would be good for me. I guess I then developed an interest to some degree. My wife thought that if I went to the library the experience would help me. We had not made any efforts to go to the library in the past.

As I walked in I was greeted by a reference librarian who had a pleasant smile. She said, "Why, Jared, you're just the man I wanted to see." This reference librarian, herself a Swiss, knew my parents. She was working at the front desk at the time. She told me that that morning a man had come in from Idaho and had brought in a large typewritten Julius Billeter book. She said she had gone through the book and had figured out that these people were related to my father.

The librarian knew that my dad wasn't feeling too well anymore as he was suffering from Parkinson's disease. She was pleased that I had come in that day, as she felt that this book should belong to my family. She suggested I take it home with me and copy the information onto family group sheets.

I was curious about this book. The librarian repeated that a man had brought it in from Idaho but that she didn't know who he was. He didn't say much about the book except that it ought to belong to someone in Salt Lake, or possibly to the Genealogical Library.

118

The librarian explained to me how to transfer the information onto family group sheets and how to figure out the relationship to all these people. I took the book home and mentioned this incident to my mother over the phone. She said, "Yes, about nineteen years ago a man borrowed that book." (We never found out whether the man who returned the book to the library was the same one who borrowed it from my parents.)

Because I had a full load in college I planned to postpone transferring the information, but for some reason I had a feeling that I ought to get started right away. At first, recording the information on family group sheets was a little difficult and I didn't particularly enjoy filling out the forms, but I got started, filled out a few sheets, and submitted them. The book contained both my direct lines and the collateral lines. I thought I would concentrate on the direct lines and not worry about the collateral lines, but since the information was there I had the feeling I should submit all the names. The book contained six thousand names. The families went from the early 1500s clear up to the end of the 1800s, and some further.

I was quite restless during the next few months. The book seemed to haunt me. A still small voice reminded me that it was my responsibility to do this work and that I needed to submit these names as soon as possible. The librarian who had turned over the book to me was also very emphatic about this work, reminding me that it was my responsibility because my father was ill.

After I had completed recording the information from the Julius Billeter book, I became quite curious about other lines and frequently went to the library and researched them. One day when I was in the library I went to the Swiss clan books. I had a definite impulse to pick up a particular book and browse through it. In this book I found an entire Ulrich line, one of my father's lines. A researcher had compiled a listing of everyone with that surname from the year 1450 through 1950. Here again were thousands of names. My wife and I saw to it that the temple work was done for all the permissible names on all these lines. The society suggested that I have most of the names placed in the temple file rather than in the family file. We ourselves performed only a few of the ordinances because of the great number. Since that time I have found other lines with thousands of names.

From this experience I got my interest in genealogy. It taught me that if a person will put forth the effort to search, the way will be opened up and he will obtain the spirit of Elijah. I know that the ancestors on the other side are then made aware of the efforts the person is making and they will keep at him constantly and urge him to continue this research work. Since that initial experience I have found many other names on various lines.

I firmly believe that in the preexistence we made a commitment to those who were to become our earthly forefathers and family that we would come down at this time to be a savior to these people, doing all the necessary research and having the temple work done for them. If we have an intense desire, the Lord will help us in this crucial work.

My Records and the Teton Dam Break

Reba Bauer

I live in the community of Wilford, less than a quarter of a mile from the Teton River along the road now commonly known as Pole Line Road. As I write (the fall of 1976), we are living in a HUD (government-furnished) trailer home on our farm. We are members of the Wilford Ward, St. Anthony Idaho Stake.

On the morning of June 5, 1976, my six-year-old granddaughter Cassie and I were at home alone. For several weeks I had had such a terrible feeling of impending disaster or tragedy that I had been praying constantly for the spiritual and physical welfare of my family. I had also previously purchased a Book of Mormon study course from the Ricks College bookstore, and as I was studying through this material I read that if we do not bear our testimonies we will lose them. I had read this before, but this time it struck me very forcefully as I thought of the very few times in my life that I had borne my testimony. Not wishing to lose it, but rather to build and strengthen it, I promised myself that next fast day would find me on my feet sharing my testimony and thanking my Heavenly Father for all the many blessings he constantly showers upon me.

On the morning of June 5 I began my fast, praying that I might have the help of the Lord in bearing my testimony on fast Sunday,

June 6. My granddaughter was playing with her new baby puppies. I was studying in the scriptures, hence we did not have the radio or television playing.

I do not know at what time my phone rang. Cassie answered it and said, "Hurry, Grandma, it's important!" It was my niece, Judy Larson. She said, "Aunt Reba, what are you doing home? The Teton Dam has broken. Get out of there quickly!"

Several years ago when my children were small, we had a bad flood in the middle of January. My husband and I did not realize the urgency of getting out quickly, so when we did try to leave we were unable to drive in our car. The water had already poured across a low spot in the road just below our home. The children and I had to climb through a fence, run through the neighbor's field behind his barnyard and onto higher ground, where my husband's uncle picked us up in a car. My husband backed our car up to higher ground, and a boat picked him up and brought him out. This was a very terrifying experience for us.

As I hung up the phone I looked at Cassie and remembered that experience. I knew that I was much older and much heavier now, and that I could not possibly run anywhere with her. I was worried because my car had not been in good running condition for some time. Frequently I could not even get it to start without jumper cables.

I grabbed Cassie's hand and we ran to the car. It started on the second attempt, and we were on our way. As we started out of the yard I realized that my bottom teeth were still soaking in a container on the kitchen cupboard. I couldn't go anywhere in public without them! I pulled over and stopped in front of my house and sent Cassie in for them while I held my foot on the gas feed. The car motor was sputtering, and I didn't know if it would keep going or stop.

As Cassie disappeared inside the door, I remembered my genealogy records — one of my most valued possessions. Should I take a chance that my car would keep going and run in the house for them, or should I leave them behind? They were very precious to me. I had spent most of my time in the past two or three months working on them so that when the Ricks College students went home I could go back to their genealogical library to do research. I could not leave my records, so I ran into the house just as Cassie was coming out. My niece and nephew, Doug and Jeannine Wright of Douglas, Arizona, had been visiting me the week before, and they had been looking through two of my books. These two books were still lying on a table in my living room as I had been doing some catch-up work in them. I ran and grabbed them, turned to leave, then remembered I had three more books full of valuable information. Two of these books had belonged to my parents and had come into my possession after their death. I laid back down on the living room table the two books I was holding, ran to the room where I kept my genealogical records, grabbed those three books and ran.

I decided I would go to the dry farm (twenty miles from our home) and tell my husband the news of the dam. I did not want to be separated from my family if it were possible to keep us together. Not yet realizing how huge this disaster would be, I thought we could go to Rexburg and stay with our son Brad and his family. Their home was situated across the street to the north of the Ricks College football field.

Somewhere along the road to the dry farm I glanced at the back seat of the car. A sick feeling came over me as I noticed that in my panic I had neglected to pick up my two books of remembrance from the livingroom table. These two books were my main books. One contained the records of all my direct ancestors as far back as they were traced — records of all the members of my family, my husband's ancestors, and members of his family. The other book contained family histories, spiritual experiences, certificates (birth, death, marriage), patriarchal blessings, newspaper clippings of weddings and other events pertaining to family members, poems I had written about my family, and many other things that were valuable to me. (I am family genealogist for my father's family, the James Farrimond Family Organization.) The book also contained many things belonging to the organization. I am somewhat of a perfectionist in record-keeping, hence along with the usual genealogical information I also had blessing dates and mission, college, and armed service information of different family members.

My records were the most complete records in the family, and I was the sole possessor of much of this information. I had also just completed writing a short biography of each of my four children, recording my recollections of them in their growing years and the things about them that made each one special to me. How sick I was to lose all of these things! I started praying and asked my Heavenly Father to please keep those materials safe.

I began to realize about that time that the flood was a major disaster. Up to that time I had thought that our house might be flooded and moved away from its foundation, but I expected to go back home after it was all over and find everything still there and most things salvageable. But now that we were far away and safe, my panic had subsided and I began to think a little more rationally. I now felt sure that our home and everything in it would be destroyed, though I did not expect that everything would disappear completely.

As we passed the White Owl Butte and pulled onto our dry farm, I could see that no one was there. (My husband had heard the news on the pickup radio and had left immediately for home. We somehow missed each other along the way.) About a mile on into the dry farm my car sputtered and died; Cassie and I were stranded. We walked and rested and walked and rested for a period of approximately three to four hours. During this time all I could think about was my genealogy. In one bedroom I had a file cabinet full of genealogical materials. In another bedroom I had a desk full of similar things. In my living room closet I had a suitcase half full of old letters and other information regarding previous research that had been done by others. I had genealogical materials scattered all over the house! I felt certain it could not all be protected, but I hoped and prayed for a miracle anyway!

124

At ten minutes to five, one of our dry farm neighbors came to check on some cattle. He brought Cassie and me back down into the valley. He said Brad's home in Rexburg was flooded, so we waited in Teton. When my husband and I were finally reunited, we drove to Tetonia, across to Ashton, and back down to St. Anthony. We probably covered around forty miles; the usual trip to St. Anthony from Teton is five miles. My name had been on the missing list and broadcast over the radio throughout the day, and my family all thought Cassie and I were drowned. At midnight when we walked into my sister's home in St. Anthony, it was a happy and thankful reunion for each of us.

On the day after the flood, my husband's cousin, Harvey Bauer, let us move into his home in St. Anthony, since he was working in Utah and his home was unoccupied. Everything we needed was there — dishes, bedding, linens, and even a few groceries. The phone was also connected. We were thankful to be alone in a house and together as a family.

A few days later a very dear friend of our family, Vera Young, called and said that a relative in Salem had found on their property a genealogical record book which belonged to a Bauer. Her son and daughter-in-law had brought it to her, and when she opened it and saw a picture of my mother and my father and their children, she knew it belonged to me. As we were talking, I remembered that the books of remembrance belonging to three of my children were stored in our home. Until then I had completely forgotten about them.

I found that the book was not mine but that of my oldest son Jeff. It was very muddy and warped. I scratched and scraped the mud off the pages and found that no pages were torn or missing. Although the book itself was not salvageable, the information was, and it seemed good to have something — anything — that had belonged to us before the flood.

A couple of weeks later another lady called and said that her husband's cousin had found a genealogy record book near his home by the Sugar City overpass. She was sure it belonged to me. My hopes were high that this time one of my books was found. I hurried to her home. This time the book, muddy and warped but intact, was the one belonging to my daughter Debbie. Once again I was thrilled to have something we had owned before the flood, regardless of condition. And again, after scraping and scratching the mud from the pages, there was more valuable information to be copied onto new sheets and put into a new book.

Up to this time I had not been physically able to go out and look for our possessions. My husband, however, had gone out searching daily, and it seemed to us that he found something belonging to almost everyone in the entire flood area except us. This was very discouraging, but I still had hopes that someone would call and say the table and my genealogy books were found somewhere high in a tree, on top of someone's roof, on top of someone's barn, on top of some bridge, or on top of the American Falls Dam!

Today I know that my genealogy books are gone. Still, each time we drive along through the flood area, I find myself searching the tree tops and along the river banks and out through the fields for some sign of my genealogical records.

But I learned from this experience. Perhaps I was so involved in writing up extra information which is valuable but not necessary, in collecting and filing newspaper clippings and other documents, and in making scrapbooks that I was forgetting and neglecting the important work of research and submitting names for temple work. Perhaps Heavenly Father allowed my memorabilia to be taken away so that I could "get my house in order" and get back to the important work of research; or perhaps I needed a lesson on the importance of keeping my records in one place instead of strewn all over the house; or perhaps I just needed to know that I could still be obedient and begin again the process of collecting and filing away the records of my people.

The genealogical information which I lost is still available to me through the two books found in the flood, through the three books I took with me in the car, and through family and church records. And with the help of family members I am once again beginning to collect new materials. Some things I lost can never be replaced, but I have not lost anything really important. I will have to spend a great deal of time redoing my records; but this may prove to be no loss at all, rather a blessing and help.

I know that miracles happen in various ways, and certainly *many* miracles have come to the victims of the Teton Dam disaster. Many things have happened to me for my benefit, such as things I have observed and thoughts that have passed through my mind which have been for my learning and spiritual growth. As tragic and disastrous as the Teton Dam break was, I am grateful to my Father in heaven that I was one of the thousands involved. The blessings which have come to me spiritually have compensated many times over for our losses. While on the dry farm that day I realized of what little value our worldly possessions really are. How quickly they can all be taken from us! How important it is that we strive for things of eternal value!

Powder-Can Genealogy

A. Boyd Nielsen

My great-grandfather Samuel McMurdie was born September 24, 1830, in London, England, the son of Robert McMurdie and Mary Ann Bill. He emigrated from England in 1853 with his parents, and he was prominent in the early history and settlement of Cedar City in Iron County and the towns of Wellsville and Paradise in Cache County.

The search for Samuel's ancestry in London has been very difficult because of the numerous Church of England parishes and nonconformist chapels there. For many years family members searched their homes for clues to help identify the exact residence of the McMurdie family in the London metropolitan area. The following story is but one of the many fascinating and inspiring incidents in our search for Samuel's ancestors.

On April 9, 1966, my uncle, Kenneth J. Nielsen, and Frank Balls were working in the "old blacksmith shop" on the Samuel I. McMurdie farm in Paradise, Utah. This farm and blacksmith shop were originally owned by Samuel McMurdie and his wife Sarah Ann Kay. While working in the shop, Uncle Ken accidentally knocked an old powder can from a shelf. As the can hit the ground its lid came open, revealing some papers inside. Uncle Ken and Frank inspected the contents and discovered that they had found some old documents pertaining to the McMurdie family during the period when the family was living in London.

I was one of the genealogists for the Samuel McMurdie Family Organization at that time, so Jennie McMurdie telephoned me as soon as she had inspected the contents of the can. I arrived at the McMurdie residence a few minutes later.

The old powder can was badly rusted and had several holes in it, but the documents it had contained for approximately a hundred years were in excellent condition. Yet I could hardly read the documents because my heart was pounding so hard with excitement. The contents of the old powder can, which are now highly treasured by all of Samuel McMurdie's posterity, provided us with a glimpse into the McMurdie family's preparations for their voyage to America. All of the documents, dated the latter part of 1852 in London, detailed transactions with various business establishments, brokers, and individuals. Also included was Samuel McMurdie's priest's license and priest's certificate. From these documents we were able to reconstruct the actual purchases made by the family to outfit themselves for the trip to Utah. From Samuel's priest's certificate from the Southwark Branch we learned that Samuel was secretary of this branch in December of 1852. From the various documents we were able to establish the approximate location of the family residence during this period.

I have had many spiritual experiences over the years that have convinced me of the divine nature of genealogy and temple work. Genealogical research has been one of the great joys of my life. I have a strong testimony of the work and testify that God hears and answers our earnest prayers for guidance in finding the records necessary to provide salvation for the dead.

Paper Treasure at the End of the Road

George Ryskamp

Some years ago I went to Spain as a student to write a paper for the Church as well as work on resources of Spanish genealogy. I had just started working on my own genealogy when an American girl named Jeri Bebout and her mother came to the Brigham Young University dormitory in Madrid. They had been down in Cullera, Valencia, with some other BYU students who were on the semester abroad program and had spent the weekend in the home of Jeri's aunt.

Jeri, her mother, and a friend named Florence Pratt had attempted to do some genealogical work in Madrid but had been unable to locate anything. Feeling very frustrated, they stopped in at the dorm to have dinner and meet some of the Church members there. We started talking. When they found that I was there doing genealogical research also, the three women decided to stay and try to find more information. They asked me if I would help in doing some genealogical research, and I agreed.

We went together to a parish called Tuejar but found that their before-1865 records had been destroyed. We eventually came to realize that in that area vast amounts of records had been burned during the Spanish Civil War. We visited about ten parishes, and of those only three had any records at all.

130

Even though the records ended in 1865, we did find that Jeri's grandmother had come from a small town called Puebla de San Miguel. We decided to travel to this town the next day and spend a few days discovering what we could.

We arrived at midday and met the secretary of the town, who happened to be a distant relation of Jeri's. We were very excited because he told us that the parish record existed as far back as the 1600s. San Miguel is just a dying farm town with a population of only seventy persons. It is about a half-hour drive from the nearest little village and is nestled in a valley surrounded by huge mountains. It is literally the end of the road.

The secretary of the town, Senor Barrachina, was very helpful and set us up in an abandoned building. The records were stored in an old cabinet, and part of the building went into the side of a hill, making it especially cold and damp. There was only one tiny electric light bulb to work by.

We dug into our work and must have worked a good five hours before we noticed that something was wrong. One of the books was missing. Without this book, which contained the records from 1700 to 1750, we were not able to use the other valuable books which dated back even further. We had reached a standstill.

We inquired what had happened to the book. Senor Barrachina informed us that during the Spanish Civil War in 1938-39 Spanish troops had gone through the area and had camped in the church. It was cold there and they shredded one of the books and used it for kindling for a fire. As it turned out, Senor Barrachina's father came in and told these soldiers they could not do that because these books were valuable. He risked his life by taking the books away from the soldiers and hid them. That was the only reason there were any books left at all.

I must admit we were all very downhearted after hearing that news, but we didn't give up. We knew that the Lord can do everything and will help his children if it is for a wise purpose. I

131

had already looked in all the more obvious sources such as the city hall newspapers. There I found a document to help me get across one of the lines, but none of the rest. We looked through some auxiliary records which were not parish records, but they were of no help either.

Because we felt that this work was important, we went to the Lord in prayer, asking him to help us know what we must do because we had reached a standstill with the records.

Jeri was working in one of the parish books from the 1800s when suddenly her eye was caught by a piece of paper lying in between two pages. She picked it up and began to read the names. They were the names of her ancestors, direct-line relatives. They were the names that would have been in the missing book. We all stopped our work and there, in that little room, wept with joy. We knew that the Lord had placed that paper there for a purpose. Because of it we were able to trace the lines clear back to the 1600s as far as the records would allow. Jeri said she had never felt the Lord's hand as strongly as she did that day, guiding and directing our every move. We copied the information on a new card and inserted it in the place where we had found it.

This is the type of experience referred to in the Words of Mormon verses 6 and 7 and in Doctrine and Covenants section 3, verse 19, where we are told about things being done for wise purposes known only to the Lord as he prepares the way for his promises to be fulfilled. As mortals we are infinitesimally small compared to the immensity of the universe, yet the Lord cares for each of his children in every estate throughout eternity.

I've come to realize through experiences I have had that the Lord will provide the means in genealogical research because there are people very much alive on the other side of the veil who need their work to be completed. This experience in Spain is a living witness of that truth.

VI

Directed by
Dreams

Question:

There have been apostles and prophets and even some lesser people in every age who have been guided by dreams. Do we dare to think that the dreams we modern people have could possibly be meaningful, even helpful, in doing our genealogical research?

Beneath a Peach Tree

Margaret Martindale

My mother's family was among the first settlers of the town of Whittier, California, a small settlement founded by the Quakers in the late eighteen hundreds. Mother's father, Dr. William Vestal Coffin, was a prominent member of the community and had part in the planning of the new town.

Association with my grandfather has had a profound effect on my life in many ways. In particular were the special experiences he shared with me. Grandfather often had dreams which foretold future events such as a sister's death or a friend's hair turning white overnight. Also he seemed to know that there was a special relationship between the two of us that had to do with the future.

One summer afternoon, when I was about ten years old, Grandfather invited me to come into the garden with him. We sat on a bench beneath the peach tree and he gave me a shoebox and asked me to open it. Inside were many items that had belonged to his mother: a tintype of an acquaintance; a little book called *Sweetness and Light*; a piece of pettipoint embroidered with the words, "Thou Hast a Friend"; Grandmother's gold hatpin, cameo, and silver thimble.

There was also a small gold Bible, its brown pages worn with constant use. Inside the back cover was pasted a small envelope.

Curiously I opened it to discover six small folded pieces of paper. Each contained a lock of hair, a name, and a birth date — one for each of Grandmother's children. Even at such a young age, I was intrigued with holding something so old.

Grandfather reached over and took my hand, saying in a very solemn voice: "Margaret, I have had a dream. One day you will be called upon to do a great religious work for our family. It will be an important work. You must do it."

As I grew older, my visits with Grandfather in Whittier became more precious to me. I recall that Grandfather spent long hours in his workroom upstairs in his big house. Sometimes there was a lady there typing for him.

Upon my graduation from Whittier College and before my teaching job commenced in September, I spent some time at the summer home of a friend at Lake Tahoe. It was during this vacation that I first heard the story of the restored gospel. My vacation was cut short, however, when I received news of Grandfather's illness. Could I come to Whittier for the month of August and help Grandmother take care of him?

I spent a lot of time sitting by Grandfather's bedside talking with him. He reminded me of the dream he had had so long ago. "Do you remember?" he asked several times. I assured him that I did, and that I would do whatever was necessary as soon as it was time to do so. Four months later, on Christmas day, Grandfather passed away.

I was baptized into The Church of Jesus Christ of Latter-day Saints two years later. About the same time, I discovered at my mother's house a box containing six typewritten volumes about Grandfather's family. I thought back to my childhood memory of Grandfather's workroom and the sound of the typewriter. I quickly glanced through each volume. There were family histories, stories of individual experiences, and many pictures. As I picked up the last volume entitled "Genealogy," I asked myself, "Did this have something to do with Grandfather's dream?"

In the years that followed I spent many wonderful hours reading about my ancestors. I studied a great deal about the plan of salvation. I learned that whenever the fulness of the gospel is on the earth, the Lord has agents to whom he gives power to bind on earth and seal eternally in the heavens. This sealing power, restored in this dispensation by Elijah the prophet, is the means whereby "all covenants, contracts, bonds, obligations, oaths, vows, performances, connections, associations or expectations, 'attain' efficacy, virtue, or force in and after the resurrection from the dead; for all contracts that are not made unto this end have an end when men are dead." (D&C 132:7.)

When it came time to do the sealing for Grandfather and Grandmother I was aware of Grandfather's presence as I participated in the ordinance. A peaceful feeling came over me, and with great joy I knew that I was doing what Grandfather had said I should. The "great religious work" for my family was under way.

It is my testimony that the spirit of Elijah was very much with Grandfather and is also now with me. His great desire was to keep his children and grandchildren aware of their ancestors. My heart in turn became filled with a great desire to go much further than awareness. I intend to take care of the ordinances which will seal my wonderful family together for all eternity.

My Brother's Message

Leslie Bushell

My first experience of feeling a closeness to my ancestors happened early in the days after I joined the Church in England. As I studied, I could see the importance of baptism as the first step towards salvation for all mankind. My heart filled with gratitude at the thought that the good Lord had prepared a way for the saving ordinances to be done vicariously and, thinking of the billions of people who had left the earth without this knowledge, its beautiful justness appealed to me.

I soon visited my parents' home and began my inquiries and research into the family tree. They assisted me as much as they could. My dad, having served as clerk of the parish council for some thirty-four years, suggested that I might find something of interest in the records he had in his possession dating back to 1707. I looked, and for most of that night I was very involved in what was recorded there.

Checking back in those records, I found the name Bushell spelled also in five other ways by different clerks down through the years (Bushel, Bushall, Bushnell, and Bishell, not to mention one entry in 1716 as Boushschelle). The dawn was breaking when I finally decided to get some sleep (the dawn breaks around 3:00 A.M. in July in England), and I was asleep as soon as my head touched the pillow.

138

In my sleep I was visited by my younger brother Keith, who had been killed during World War II while flying on a mercy mission over the sea. He took me by the hand and we moved upward, passing before our ancestors. We passed my grandparents, who were dead, my great-grandparents, great-great-grandparents, and so on until there were literally thousands who stood before us. So vividly did they appear that I could assess and distinguish the pecularities of their features and easily recognize the paternal and maternal families.

When I awoke after five hours I was humbly aware of my obligations to my ancestors, who had made it possible for me to be here in this dispensation of time. I began my search for their records right away.

I have a testimony of the spirit of Elijah in genealogical work and am sure that when we are so engaged we draw near to those of our ancestors who have accepted the gospel in the spirit world and who need our help in their progression.

Fulfillment of a Blessing

Xavier L. Tuttle

My great-aunt, Mary Franklin Thompson, was the first to join the Church in our family. She was baptized in Nashville, Tennessee, in 1909. Aunt Mary died in 1942.

Some time later, she came to me in a dream with a small baby in her arms. She told me that if I would get her temple work done, she would help me with my genealogical research. So I did the temple work for all her family, including her infant son whose record I found in the family Bible.

After I had done their work, the rest of the Franklin family records opened up to me like a book and I was able to get the records and have the work completed back to the immigrant ancestors who came to Maryland in 1634.

My brother, Hilary Howse Lingner, died the year before I married (1939). He was twenty-four years of age. It was after my fifth child had started school that I began having dreams of my brother Hilary coming to me. It happened night after night (about five in the morning, actually). He seemed to be standing by my bed, dressed in the gray suit he was buried in. I could see him as clearly as if he were alive. I always got the impression that he wanted something but I did not know what.

In another of my dreams Hilary had just died and my mother and I were at the mortuary. My mother was taking his death terribly hard, just as she had when it actually happened. For some reason I did not feel at all sad; in fact, I felt happy within myself. As we left the mortuary the area was like a large field of tree stumps where trees had been sawed down. My brother's voice seemed to be coming to me from the ground, pleading that he needed my help. He said he could do nothing without my help.

I awakened troubled by the dream and wondered about the meaning of it so much that I was impressed to write it down so as not to forget it. It was at this time that I began to realize he wanted me to get his temple work done.

At another time I dreamed we were having a family get-together. There was a multitude of people; I was dishing up salad from a very large bowl and there was only one large helping left. I was very tired and hungry. My brother Hilary came and took what was left. He said to me, "You've had your chance, and now it is my turn." I woke up crying.

I feel that this dream had a very significant meaning. I was working on our genealogy, but instead of submitting for temple work the sheets for which I had all the information, I was spending my time trying to get information on ancestors much further back. After this dream, I submitted all the sheets I could of my nearest and closest relatives who had died.

I had only one other dream of Hilary coming to me and that was a long time afterwards. He asked to see my book of remembrance. He took it and sat down in an old armchair that belonged to my grandfather. Hilary turned the pages very slowly, studying each sheet. When he had finished he gave the book back to me and said that what I had done was both complete and correct, but that I should continue to do this work. "There are many others waiting for you to help them," he said.

Later I dreamed I was in an open car going very slowly through a town. There were others in the car but I didn't know who they were. Everywhere I looked there were crepes on the doors of homes. (When I was a child in the South, on the doors of the homes where someone had died, crepes (or wreaths) were hung, usually made of white lilies with large bows at the top and long streamers hanging down.)

When we got out of town the car stopped. A multitude of people was there to meet me, all happy to see me. They were clamoring for my help. One man stood out from all the rest of the crowd, a tall, thin man with fair complexion and light brown hair. He was very handsome on one side of his face, but the other side had a terrible scar that covered almost the whole side of his face.

Once when my mother was here visiting I wanted her help with genealogy, so I decided to tell her of my dreams of Hilary. I bore to her my testimony of this work for the dead. When I told her of the man with the scarred face, she cried and said that that man was her grandfather, Samuel Franklin. He had had cancer of the face.

She went on to tell me that she had always felt I had some special mission to perform because my life was preserved at birth. I was a seven-month baby and weighed only two pounds and three ounces.

Several times I tried to get genealogical information from Aunt Georgia Lingner Newsom, my father's sister, but she died before I could get any records from her. About a month after she died her son, Grover, Jr., whom I hadn't heard from since I was a child, wrote me a letter saying, "I don't know why, but I feel very much impressed to send you the family records."

A year after I received the family records from my cousin, I dreamed I was in the kitchen preparing dinner when my mother came in. She casually sat down and said, "Xavier, Georgia is ready for her work to be done."

With the information I had received from my cousin, Grover Jr., I am happy to say I was able to do the temple work for Aunt

142

Georgia, Uncle Grover, and my grandparents and great-grandparents.

I have been asked, "Why did your brother come to you and not to someone else to do this work?"

I received my patriarchal blessing the morning after I married. In it I was told that before I was born, in the preexistence, those who would become my ancestors chose me to do this work. I was also told that I would have the Holy Ghost to guide me, and that if I will do my full duty in this respect, when I pass to the other side the meeting will be one of rejoicing on the part not only of my ancestors but also of the Lord.

I bear testimony that temple work and genealogy are part of the Lord's work here on earth and are necessary for our salvation in the highest degree in the celestial kingdom. I would like to urge everyone doing this work for the dead to first do all that is at hand and is easy to do and not to put it off for what is still lacking. After doing all you can, the Holy Ghost will aid you in getting information that now seems impossible to obtain.

My Mother's Concern

Leila M. Beck

One night during the winter of 1929, in my sleep I thought I heard and answered a telephone ring. The call was from my mother, Clara Ann (Huish) Moore, who had been dead two years. She told me that my father, Samuel D. Moore, wanted to go to the temple but could not find his temple clothes. My mother told me where everything was to be found. She also told me that in the bottom of her trunk were the records of the family of her mother, Ann (Smith) Huish. These records of her forefathers were in a white, homemade purse. There were also many letters from England that would help in the search for the records of those who were dead.

I was further told that it was my duty to compile these records, send them to the temple, and see that all the ordinances and sealings were completed. My mother told me that she was in the St. George Temple. When I started telling her about my family and the things going on at home, she said: "Leila, I am too busy and have not time for that. Do as you are told. I must go now." At that, up went the receiver.

As I called to her, "Oh Mother, Mother," my words woke my husband, J. Milton Beck. He asked what the matter was, and I told him what had happened. The incident of the telephone call

144

was so real that I could not go back to sleep that night. At the time we didn't even have a phone in our home, or I would have wondered if I hadn't actually talked to mother, it seemed that real. I was thrilled to know that our loved ones were so close and watching over us.

The next morning I could hardly wait to get my husband off to work and the children off to school so that I could go to my father. My son Milton accompanied me on his way to school as far as my father's house. When I reached his home I opened the door and was surprised to see him sitting at the table crying. He wiped the tears away quickly and said, "Leila, what brings you here so early in the morning?" I told him about the dream and Mother's saying that he wanted to go to the temple but could not find his temple clothes. Father told me he had come home from a water meeting about 11:30 P.M. the previous evening and, sure enough, Wayland Whightman had asked him to go with him to the Salt Lake Temple the next day. But he could not find where Mother had put his temple clothes! While searching for them he had felt Mother's presence and thought he saw her.

I told him that part of his things were pressed between the pages of a large book in a trunk, while the rest were in the wardrobe. He said he had already looked in both places, but when we went in together and looked we found everything just where Mother had told me they were. Father left that afternoon for Salt Lake City and remained there for several weeks doing temple work.

On Father's return he gave me the records in the old English purse so that I could begin my work and get the names ready to be sent to the temple. I told my sister about all this and she told a skeptical friend, who said, "That was just a dream, and when she sends the records in she will find that the work is all done." But when the names were sent in to be checked by the Genealogical Society for temple work, not one name had been done, and we had the privilege of doing the names in the temple ourselves.

When all the other ordinances were done, we had the sealing work performed in the Manti Temple.

I want to bear my testimony that it is up to us to do the work for our own dead and give them an opportunity to progress. I know that our loved ones are watching over us and that they expect us to live our lives so that we may go into the temples and do that vital work of salvation for ourselves and our dead kindred.

Prompted to Act

Halvar Wallin

I was born in Sweden in 1917 of good parents who were poor materially but who had faith in Christ. They had never heard of the restored gospel. As a child I attended the Baptist Sunday School where my parents had membership, but I never got things straight in my mind how God, who filled the whole universe, could still be so small that he could dwell in the heart of a man. This and other Protestant beliefs were nothing but confusion to me.

A few things happened between 1951 and 1955 that changed my way of life. First, my mother died after suffering from cancer for ten years. She was very close to me because I was like her in many ways, and I missed her very much. Then, in 1953 I had an unusual dream. In it I saw my mother in a little boat out on a lake sitting there without a sail, oars, or motor; and she couldn't get anywhere. I yelled out to her that I would come and save her, but someone told me that I couldn't because I didn't have what I needed to help her. When I awakened I was very puzzled. I never forgot that dream.

Later that same year my wife and I traveled in the United States for ten weeks. Salt Lake City was our last stop, where we visited some old friends who had become "crazy Mormons."

During our trip I took hundreds of slides, especially during our week-long stay in Salt Lake City, a place I found very beautiful. I decided that if I had to live in the United States, this would be the only place I could live. When all of my films were developed I found, to my great sorrow, that all the pictures that had been taken during the week in Salt Lake were ruined. They were just black — not one had turned out.

Later I was asked to show some pictures and talk about our trip to the United States for the Vasa Orden Club, of which my wife and I were members. I thought of our friends we had stayed with in Salt Lake, who had thousands of beautiful slides of that area, so I wrote and asked them if I might borrow a few to show to the club. They sent me about 275 slides and asked me to show them also to their friends in the Mormon chapel in my home town. I agreed to do this, but it took me a long time before I got around to it.

One day I stopped at the chapel and told the story of my friends in Salt Lake and about the slides. Two young missionaries met me and said they would invite all the members to MIA on Tuesday night to see the pictures.

At the end of our first program one of the missionaries asked me if they could come to my home and tell my wife and me more about the Church. I said yes, but it was only because I did not have a better answer or an excuse ready at that time. The missionaries gave us the lessons within the next two months. After the first one I knew that what they told us was the true gospel and God's plan of salvation for his children. It was so simple that I felt as if I had known it all before. Baptism was set for my wife, myself, and two of our three daughters of age. The mission president, among others, planned to attend our baptism.

But one week before our baptism my wife and I were very troubled by the decision we had made. We had a good retail business in our town of fifty thousand inhabitants and most of the people knew us very well. Besides that, all soccer fans in Sweden knew me as a popular soccer star. I feared I would lose my following if I joined the Church; also, I knew that many of our customers would stop patronizing our store. The name *Mormon* was a bad word in people's minds because of false stories which had been circulated about this religion and the Mormon people.

My wife and I decided to write a letter to the mission president and the elders who had taught us the gospel. In the letter I put together a lot of what I felt were good excuses and said that we felt we were not ready to take the step yet. The same Friday morning when I was going to take the letter to the mail box, we got a letter from my father. This was a very unusual thing, because he lived just a half-hour drive from our home and we used to drive out and see him every other weekend. I thought that something special must have happened in our family to cause him to write a letter.

Hurriedly I read the letter and was stunned by the message: "Dear son, if you ever find a way back to your Heavenly Father, don't hesitate to take that way." At that moment I felt as if the Lord was standing in front of me and telling me, "You stupid fellow, how many times do I have to call on you?" My father had no chance of knowing that we were investigating the Church, because we kept that fact to ourselves, to our immediate family. If he had known, he would have warned us against the Mormons, for he had heard nothing but bad things about them. I am convinced my Father in heaven used him as a tool.

When my "paralyzed" body started to function again I took the letter meant for the mission president and tore it to pieces. We were all baptized on the day that was set, and we have never regretted it. That was the moment our life really began.

As I learned of the priesthood and temple work, the dream of my mother returned to me and immediately I started to search for my ancestors and my wife's ancestors. It has been a wonderful blessing to know that as a result of this search between eight and nine hundred souls have had a chance to embrace the gospel in the spirit world through our proxy temple work for them. This must have been the reason why the Lord called on us two, the only members of the Church from either of our families since the restoration of the gospel.

149

A Samoan with Russian Ancestry

Sipuao J. Matuauto

Catherine II, known as Catherine the Great, and Nicholas II and his wife and family all appeared to me with my mother in a dream in the fall of 1976. In the dream I was told that these white people were my mother's relatives and I was supposed to help them, but at the time I was given no knowledge as to their true identity. My mother told me in the dream that I had only forty-five minutes to help these people who came with her. My mother had died on April 2, 1964. She and my father were devout Mormons.

After my mother and her white relatives appeared to me in the dream, I learned from the Spirit that these people had accepted the gospel and desired to have their temple work done. I greatly desired to commence a search for information about these people right away, for the time my mother gave me to get this task done was so short, only forty-five minutes, not even an hour!

As much as I wanted to start immediately, I had no idea where to begin my search. Sensing a barrier like a wall before me, I went down on my knees to the Lord. I pleaded with the Lord: "If it's possible, please give me more details about these white people who appeared to me with my mother in the dream, so that I may be able to help them and get their temple work done." I told the Lord that I was willing to do all I could to help them out but I

150

desperately needed more details about them. I wanted to know who they were and where they came from.

As a result of my fervent and earnest prayers, I had another dream two or three days after the first dream. In the second dream, more information was given to me. I was taken to a land I have never before seen, and as I walked on a deserted street that went uphill in this land I saw a white man standing nearby. He was dressed like a peasant and looked unshaven. Upon seeing this man I started speaking Russian, and immediately he smiled and came towards me. We greeted each other joyfully and conversed in Russian. For at least ten minutes I conversed with him. I understood that it was Russian I was speaking fluently, as if I were a native. At the end of the conversation, I said to him in Russian that I was a descendant of the czars.

Immediately after I had said this I woke up. I sat on my bed reliving in my mind the dream I just had. The dream had also made clear to me that the white people who appeared to me in my first dream as my mother's relatives were Russian.

In real life I know no word of Russian, nor have I known anything about Russia except that it is a country of communism, which I detest.

On the day after my second dream, I commenced my search. I went with a Polish friend to the University of Utah Library and checked out four books on Russia. One of these was volume one of the *History of Russia*. I took these books home and started reading them.

Without knowing why, I became very interested to read volume one of the history. As I quickly scanned through the pages, I became attracted to the reign of the Romanov czars. As I read along, the material became more and more interesting. When I came to Peter the Great, my heart felt a piercing joy. Light of understanding burst into my mind with an assurance that Peter the Great would lead me to the white people whom I was seeking. I jumped around in my apartment from joy because I received confirmation from the Spirit that Peter the Great was my lead. For reasons unknown to me, love was swelling inside me for this man, Peter the Great. I studied him faithfully and ended up loving him greatly in spite of his evilness.

Peter the Great led me to Peter III, one of his grandsons, who married Catherine II. As I searched faithfully for the parents of Peter III, I could not find anything about them. I began to feel a little frustrated but did not give up. I felt inspired to check about Catherine II, his wife, in the hope that something might come up there. In the library I started looking into volume C of Encyclopedia Americana.

As I looked through the pages for the name of Catherine II, I came to a picture of the woman who came to me in my first dream as my mother. You see, my mother in the dream didn't look quite like my mother. This woman was a big, tall white woman and her face looked somewhat like my mother, particularly in the manner that she wore her hair, but she wouldn't smile and she walked like a dignitary. Anyway, the picture of Catherine II in the Encyclopedia Americana looked exactly like the woman who led the group of white people in the dream. I stared at the picture and I couldn't believe I was seeing the same woman. The only difference was that Catherine smiles in the picture and she did not in the dream. In the dream she was wearing a white and pink floral dress.

I stared at the picture of Catherine for at least half an hour. I was amazed; I couldn't believe this would happen to me. I received the testimony of the Spirit that she was indeed the woman I saw in the dream who came as my mother; for she was truly one of my great-grandmothers. (She would be about a sixth great-grandmother of my mother and this would make her my seventh great-grandmother.)

After this, I started reading more about her life. She had committed much evil in this life, I discovered, but nevertheless I began at the same time to feel great love for her. I can now truly say that in spite of all the evil she had committed, I still love her very, very much. I can only pray that the Lord will forgive her.

As I studied about her life, I felt that probably some of the talents I have came from her through my mother. The talent allowing me to sing in the great Mormon Tabernacle Choir no doubt came from her. I feel strongly that I also inherited from her my love and appreciation for arts, education, and several other great things of life that are not Polynesian. I feel grateful to my ancestors, for each of them has contributed something in me. I feel that I owe them a great deal because of this.

I learned that Catherine II and Peter III had one son named Paul. Paul had three sons — Alexander I, Constantine Pavlovich, and Nicholas I. Alexander became Czar of Russia after he murdered his father Paul; Alexander I did not have any children, and upon his death his brother Constantine Pavlovich would normally have succeeded him; Constantine, however, renounced his rights to the throne in favor of his younger brother Nicholas.

Nicholas I had a son who became Czar Alexander II after the death of his father. Alexander II's oldest son Alexander III became czar upon the death of his father. Alexander III's oldest son became Nicholas II, the last czar of Russia.

The next day I borrowed volumes A and N of a set of World Book Encyclopedia to look up the three Alexanders and the two Nicholases. After finding and recording the information about the three Alexanders, I turned to volume N to look up Nicholas I and II. Across the page from the entry for Nicholas I was a picture. When I looked at it, I was amazed! There in this picture were the same girls, woman, man, and boy whom I had seen in my first dream, the people who came to me as my mother's relatives.

I sat and stared at these people in the picture. I looked at the caption underneath the picture and found there this information: Nicholas II, last czar of Russia and his family. The picture was taken six months before the czar was forced to renounce the throne. According to the article, the family was executed on July 17, 1918.

My heart felt so touched, and tears rolled down my cheeks as the Spirit witnessed to me, "These are the people who came to you for your help!" Within five days I had found all the people who had come seeking my help. During those five days I had had no sleep, night and day, because I had been given only forty-five minutes to get their work done! I didn't even feel tired during those five days while searching for information.

On the following Monday I called the Genealogical Society and asked if any work for the dead had been done on Russian lineages. I was told that very little had. Further inquiry revealed that there was a family group sheet for Nicholas II and his family in the Society's files, and I obtained a copy of it. I then felt inspired to make an appointment with a highly placed official of the Genealogical Society.

Wednesday morning came and I went to see this brother. I related to him the series of dreams I had had and the names of the people in the dreams. He then called on a staff worker to locate a family group sheet for Nicholas II and his family and also one for the family of Peter III and Catherine II. When these sheets were brought in, they indicated that temple work for Nicholas and his family was partially complete, while all the work had been done for Catherine. After a more precise check by the Royalty Identification Section, however, it was discovered that still more work could be done for Nicholas II and his family, and that in fact no work at all had been done for Catherine II! I emphasized to the official that it was important to have the work done right away, no matter who stood as proxies, because the spirits were anxiously waiting, and that in the dream Catherine had appeared quite upset. Later the Genealogical Society confirmed to me that everything necessary was being done to see that the work was completed right away.

Interestingly, the time it took for me to explain the experiences and to get the wheels turning for the temple work to be completed was *forty-five minutes!*

I truly know that searching for our ancestors is crucial to their salvation as well as to ours. I know also that if we have the kind of faith that can make miracles happen our ancestors on the other side can appear to us and let us know what they want us to do for them.

There was absolutely no way for me to locate these ancestors. Records concerning white people's migration to the Samoan Islands, in common with other genealogical records there, were very poorly kept. Generally no records at all were kept until the white missionaries came to the islands. But I have been assured by the Spirit that my mother is a descendant of Constantine Pavlovich. One of his great-grandchildren found his way to Samoa and married my mother's grandmother. Nicholas II and my mother are fourth or fifth cousins. My relationship to Nicholas II and his family is collateral, but I probably am the only relative who can help them in mortality.

I have found myself loving these people; they truly are my relatives, and I know and feel their love and appreciation for me. Without a doubt our loved ones on the other side can communicate with us if we live right, have the true desire to help them, rely upon the Lord for the information we cannot find, and are humble and trusting as we approach him for that help.

Get Started

Ervin S. McDonald

My relationship to my father and to my ancestors was made emphatically important to me by a dream that I had on May 20, 1954. I will first mention a circumstance that occurred previous to the dream, since it was significant to decisions and promises that were to follow.

Early one Saturday morning a land broker, looking at two lots east of our home in San Francisco, saw me preparing my tools to do a repair job. Thinking I was a builder, he asked if I would like to purchase those construction sites. "Yes," I replied, since I had expressed my thoughts to my wife and others that I would like to have those two lots so that I could build homes. He quoted a price for the property — low for that time, and a price which would sound ridiculously low in these times.

My mind was intent on how my wife and I could increase our holdings and have a better home. I thought this the chance of a lifetime, so I told the man I would consider the purchase and discuss it with my family and contact him on the phone. He warned me that I would have to make a decision very soon, since lots were in great demand.

A few days later I had the dream. In it I was making forms for concrete foundations on the two lots. As I paused in my work to evaluate my progress, I looked up and saw my father and a companion approaching me. The companion, I have assumed since that time, was my brother John. He died June 15, 1906, about five months after I was born. I first accepted him as a member of the family at the moment of the dream, for I had grown up without him.

My father embraced me. As he died on December 20, 1920, it had been a long time since I had seen him. I felt that heavenly love we had for each other more at that moment than at any previous time in my life; a love so great and pure that it can't be described in words. If there was ever any doubt in my mind concerning Father's love for me, that doubt has never entered my mind since my dream of that embrace.

I told Father that I knew why he had come, as I had dreamed the night before of his coming to see me about our genealogy. (*That* dream was a dream within *this* dream!) Father told me that he did want research to move faster. He said he had endeavored to get more done, but so far had not accomplished his desires. I excused the delay, as I felt that my daily routine labors and Church duties prevented me from being anxiously engaged in doing work for our family dead. I felt guilty that I had waited for a spirit messenger to get me started. A scripture flashed through my mind — "Blessed are they that have not seen, and yet have believed." (John 20:29.) The guilt, however, did not diminish my joy in seeing my father.

He answered me, "If you get started, you will be all right." Another scripture flashed through my mind: ". . . the Lord giveth no commandments unto the children of men, save he shall prepare a way for them that they may accomplish the thing which he commandeth them." (1 Nephi 3:7.)

I promised Father that I would get started on research which would lead to complete family unity through God's eternal plan and family organizations. He then asked that by the next evening I write the things he had told me and the promise I had made. As he started to leave me, I called and asked if it would be possible for him or other messengers to bring names to us. He turned, smiled, and said, "If you get started, you will be all right." John remained by my side a few more seconds and gave me a final admonition to prepare these instructions, as I might need them on the following Sunday. (That was odd. The next Sunday was fast Sunday and I suppose he expected me to tell of my dream in testimony meeting. I did *not*. But I did give a report of it at our family reunion.)

I awoke and arose. The time was 4:15 A.M. I knew that my time in the evening was taken by a night course I was teaching, so I started preparing by skimming through the book *The Way to Perfection*, reading chapter 36 carefully. (I recommend this chapter to my children and to all LDS youth.) Now I was preparing for the rest of my life. I did not buy the lots, for that would surely mean I would be too busy to do research.

Father was not accustomed to telling his children three times to do a thing, but in this very short visit he did tell me three times to get started on research. I did get started. It is my testimony that the work I am doing is most important.

Soon I was cooperating with my sisters Emily and Leona and other brothers and sisters and other family organization members to reactivate the objectives of the organization. Also, we organized the Williams families and the Briggs families to accomplish the work on those lines. It is my desire that every family member work to belong to our eternal families.

Since that time we have added dozens of names to our pedigree charts and have submitted thousands of names for temple ordinance work.

In this work I have found that the first of the many necessary steps is simply to *get started*.

VII

Help from
Those Beyond

Question:

Brigham Young said that the Prophet Joseph Smith appeared and gave him instruction several times after Joseph's death. Because of a particularly unusual circumstance in my genealogy, I feel that I need help from the other side, but no one has come to me. Are there examples of "ordinary" people receiving this kind of help?

I'll Always Remember

Rena Mills

January 7, 1965 — I'll always remember that day, for that was the day I was supposed to die. I was returning home from a visit to my parents, a short distance of 120 miles. My husband was driving and my twenty-three-month-old daughter was asleep on my lap. It started to snow when we were halfway home, but we decided to push on through what was later called "the worst blizzard of the year."

We had traveled twenty-two miles further on snowpacked, slick roads when a forceful gust of wind pushed our truck into the path of a lumber truck. We really didn't have a chance. My daughter died instantly as she was thrown into the dashboard, and my husband died eighteen hours later in the hospital. I should have died, too. I suffered from shock for four days, eighty-four fractures, and a bruised heart, besides cuts and bruises. I lay in the hospital grieving over my loss and wondering why I wasn't taken. Thank God for my faith; it is all that saved me.

As a child I had been sent to the nearby Baptist Church on Sunday. My parents said that when we children were old enough we would be allowed to join any church of our choice — any church, that is, except the Catholic Church or the Latter-day Saint Church, my father said.

161

My older brother had married when I was five years old and had been baptized into the LDS Church several years later, before my father had been so definitely set against it.

When my younger sister was twelve she decided she wanted to be baptized as a Baptist. My father was thrilled with her decision. I wanted to please my father too, so several months after my sister's baptism I was also baptized into the Baptist Church. I had doubts and felt uncomfortable in my decision, but I went ahead anyway. I longed to attend church with my Mormon friends, but I feared my father's reaction.

Before long I left the Baptists and regularly attended the Latter-day Saint Church, even though I sometimes felt guilty for having gone against my father's wishes. I was happier attending the Latter-day Saint Church and soon felt at peace. I fell in love and became engaged to a Mormon boy who was an elder in the Church and four years older than I. I was baptized January 6, 1962, and my father attended the ceremony to see my brother baptize and confirm me a member of the Church.

I was married in June 1962 at the ward chapel because the Church recommended that I not be married in the temple until I had been a member for one year. We were very happy those few short years my husband and I spent together. We were sealed in the Salt Lake Temple in October 1963 and had our six-month-old daughter sealed to us as well. Nine months later we received what we always considered to be our temple marriage gift from God — a tiny baby girl. She was only allowed to stay with us three short days before she returned to live with God, a perfect spirit too innocent to remain here on earth, but waiting for us to raise her in the Millennium.

Five months after our daughter was returned to heaven, the accident occurred and my husband and oldest daughter were taken too. Shortly after I was released from the hospital I saw them in my room one night. They stood across the room, not far from my bed. They were surrounded by a light that seemed to

162

radiate from within their being. They did not stand on the floor but several inches above, as though they were floating. In their adult spirit form my daughters looked beautiful. The oldest had long, flowing light brown hair down her back, and she was tall and slender. The younger daughter was shorter and more plump, with short curly locks of darker brown hair. My husband looked just as he had on our wedding day, one lock of his hair falling over his forehead as it always did. He spoke to me, reassuring me that they were all happy and that they missed me and would wait for me. He then told me to go on with my life on earth, as God had chosen that I remain to finish work that needed to be done.

After this vision I began to wonder just what work I needed to do. I finally decided that the genealogical research I had begun in the last year before the accident must be part of the work I had been chosen to do. I am a first-generation convert, and no one had done any ordinance work for my ancestors.

I began to write to relatives and to question my parents about their family past and present, but it wasn't until 1968 that I began in earnest to research my family genealogy.

The success I have had and the number of persons that have had their ordinance work done because of my research have been a testimony to me of my husband's words in that vision. I was chosen to be given the responsibility of our ancestors' temporal ordinances.

I have married again and have three lovely daughters to raise in God's church. One has been baptized and confirmed by my brother. My sister has now joined the Church, and my brother baptized her too. In January 1975 my parents were baptized into the Church by my brother, then in September 1976 they were sealed for time and eternity in the Provo Temple. My brother and I were sealed to our parents at that time. The Spirit that filled that sealing room as my parents joined hands and my brother and I joined hands to be sealed to them was sweet; I felt a heavenly presence there.

163

I know that the Church is true and that God sent some of us here for the purpose of helping lost souls who did not hear or accept salvation while they were alive. I know that God watches over his children and helps them when they seek his help.

I had been researching for about eight years for the family of my third great-grandmother without success. The younger children were listed in the 1870 and 1880 censuses, but since the father had died in 1866, I could not find information on him or confirm the ages of his oldest children. I did find the names of twelve children in his estate records, but no ages; and my second great-grandmother had passed on the information that she was one of sixteen children.

I tried to read the 1860 census but could not make out the writing. I looked for the family in the 1850 census for Adams and Hancock County, Illinois, but couldn't find them. A friend told me to search the 1860 census under the old number but I thought this a waste of time as the reason they had redone the films was that the first ones were too dim to read.

One day when my husband was home from work and could care for our children, I decided to go to the library to do research. I gathered up my materials and caught the bus to town. I went prepared to research another branch of the family, and when I arrived I went to the card catalog for the numbers of films I wanted. As I looked for a film reader, a voice in my head kept whispering, "Why don't you check out that old film number?" I argued with myself but finally decided to find the film and look at it. I reasoned that since it would be too dim to read I could soon get it off my mind and go on to other things.

I located the old film and placed it on the reader, but before I even tried to read it I bowed my head in prayer. I asked God's guidance and help in finding this family and getting their ordinance work done. Then I turned the machine on and began to search the dim film. I was able to read it well enough that almost immediately I found the family I had been looking for. Some of

164

the names were unreadable, so I got the new film number and between the two films was able to fill out a family group sheet, adding three more names I did not have before and the ages of the father and the older children. I then decided to search the 1850 film again to see if I could locate them on the old film. They were there, and I don't know why I wasn't able to find them on that film before. This film confirmed the findings of the 1860 census and gave me the age of an older son who married before 1860 and thus did not appear on that census with the family.

I have felt that this was one of my greatest successes. It was as if the Holy Ghost was looking over my shoulder to guide me in my endeavor. This was another proof to me that doing genealogical research is one of the reasons I was left here on earth.

Heavenly Housework

Nola R. Griffith Borrowman

I had been working on genealogy steadily for several weeks with a fierce determination to "get *somewhere*" on my father's genealogy. During these several weeks my husband was at sea. None of our young children were old enough to take on a great deal of responsibility around the house, though they did have their individual chores.

On one particular night I had been working quite hard to get some genealogical research done on my father's line. Dinner was hastily prepared and the children put to bed. I worked late that night, and finally about one in the morning I decided I was going to have to put the genealogy away, do the evening dishes and go to bed. But when I went in to do the dishes I found them already done and the kitchen cleaned up. None of the children had done it, and my husband *couldn't* have!

Over the next several weeks as I worked on the genealogy many things were mysteriously done around the house. Beds were made; dusting, dishes, and vacuuming were done. I can recall one day in particular I was downstairs with my daughter when we heard the vacuum cleaner going upstairs. When we checked upstairs, we could not find the vacuum cleaner, but the vacuuming was done. The cleaner turned out to be downstairs in the closet where it belonged. It was startling.

166

One event followed another and it became almost more than I could cope with emotionally. Dishes were done, dusting was done, beds were made, and floors were swept. It seemed that there was a small voice to tell me when the stew was done, when the baby's bottle was at the right temperature, or which way to go around the block to check on my children. My time was conserved for me at every task!

These miraculous occurrences continued for some time, until I decided that I just couldn't take the overpowering experience of receiving such mysterious help any longer. I have to admit that I put the genealogy away for a while.

Even when I wasn't busy on Father's line though, things that I had put into motion were still active. For instance, I had been writing to Aunt Dora, my father's sister, to try to get more information about Father's family. Finally she persuaded Grandfather's youngest brother's wife to write to me. She told me that she had the family Bible, but that she didn't want to part with it. She said that it had names and dates and that she would try to get someone to copy them for me, as it was too much for her to try to do.

Aunt Dora assured me that she had letters containing all the family genealogy; also deeds and other papers. I was welcome to all this information but Aunt Dora was too feeble to gather it up for me. I kept writing and seemed to get bits and pieces of information, but it was incomplete and her letters would come sometimes only once a month.

When Navy orders came for us to move, I earnestly prayed that before we went I would get the information I needed. Still no letter came. Our belongings were packed and the movers were expected the next day. Hope was growing thin.

At almost the last moment the mailman came with a box for me from Aunt Dora. Dora's son Bill was cleaning out his parent's house and moving them to a rest home. Aunt Dora insisted that the drawers full of "trash" be sent to me along with the family

167

Bible. There were tintypes of two generations of families, along with papers enough to start a family history. I had really worked hard for nearly ten years to gather this much genealogy and there it was, the day before we were to leave the Hawaiian Islands at the end of my husband's tour of duty there. Had it arrived one or two days later it could either have been lost in the forwarding or have been months catching up to us.

I surely believe that my dear deceased father could influence his sister to send me the family records. How he also arranged the help with my housework I don't know, but along with my gratitude I'm a great deal amused. He always did have a great sense of humor.

Dead Leaves

Doris Cook

One autumn day my husband was doing genealogical research in a small village church in Suffolk, England. The sun was streaming through the stained-glass window of the church vestry onto the table at which he was sitting as he searched the parish registers. He could hear the rustle of the dead leaves outside, but he was engrossed in his search and concentrating on the job at hand.

For no apparent reason his eyes wandered to the door. To his surprise he saw a mist coming from under the door, yet the sun was still shining. He did not pay too much attention to this, however, and continued with his searching.

As he worked he began to feel that he was not alone. He again raised his eyes from the book and was aware that the mist was thicker and had begun to encircle him. As he looked, he could see the outlines of people — men, women, and children — all dressed in clothes of a bygone age, gliding past him in the mist. He noticed a happiness about them, for they smiled and nodded their heads toward him as if they were pleased with what he was doing.

Then the mist faded away and he continued his work as before, the sun shining, and the dead leaves rustling outside.

169

"Railroaded"

Graham R. Mitchell

Railroading has been my life. Being a locomotive engineer for many years, I have often had occasion to travel throughout the country. Later, I worked at the state capitol for over nineteen years as a legislative representative for all of the railroads, a position of much responsibility.

After becoming a member of The Church of Jesus Christ of Latter-day Saints, my desire to learn more of the history of my own family grew day by day. I made it a point whenever possible to visit some of the areas of my boyhood. My wife, Edi, and I arranged several railroad trips through the south to Texas, Tennessee, Georgia, the Carolinas, and Virginia. We visited old homesites, cemeteries, courthouses, historical societies, monuments, and so forth.

During our travels we met many wonderful people who opened their hearts and their homes to us in true "southern hospitality." Some of our happiest moments have come through continued correspondence with these good folks in which we have recalled meaningful times shared together.

Though in the beginning I did not even know my grandmother's full name, with each year of research my genealogical family increased in number. Many books and records came into

170

my hands, some in unusual ways. As the years passed, my collection of records and correspondence became formidable in size. Many names were processed for temple work, and we felt joy in tasks accomplished.

As my retirement approached, however, it became increasingly difficult to find sufficient time for research. Gradually my genealogical efforts came to a standstill, with only an occasional letter to buoy our spirits. I promised myself that after retirement I would begin again, but each day seemed to slip by and the genealogy went unnoticed. My retirement day came and went, but still other duties seemed more pressing.

One night I was awakened by a quiet yet penetrating voice which said to me: "Brother Mitchell, you have the time; you have the opportunity; you have the information. Now get up and *do* something." Believe me, I *did!*

As one who for years had "railroaded" legislation, I was familiar with the tactics now being used by my people beyond the veil. They had ascertained the situation and were telling me exactly what to do. *I* was the one being "railroaded" to resume my genealogical responsibilities once again.

The very next day Edi and I, with the help of a friend (whom I "railroaded"), began a concentrated effort to put our genealogy in order and gather any new information necessary. Intensive library research, as well as another trip to the south, opened up many new names for us. Just three months later it was our privilege to participate in some of the temple work for my people. The balance of the temple work for the dead was completed while Edi and I served a mission in New Zealand.

We have a strong testimony of the gospel and have found great joy in serving the Lord in whatever assignment we have been called to. We have experienced the Lord's help many times as we have been faithful to the gospel. We love the genealogy work and know that it is true.

Our Russian Responsibility

Bill and Jacqueline Kaline

Bill's Introduction

Mama and Papa Kalinchenko were faithful servants of the Lord. They were Russian Baptists, converted from the Orthodox Church. Mom had many dreams of a spiritual nature. One in particular recurred each night for a month or two. She dreamed that terrible changes were going to happen in Russia, far worse than the country had thus far experienced. These dreams occurred during the Bolshevik Revolution, when the country was already in turmoil.

Mama felt impressed to tell Papa, her brother and sister, and their families of the recurring dream; but they rejected her spiritual message and told her that Russia would soon be better and that they would not leave. Still Mama felt that the Lord wanted them to go to America.

Mama was persistent, the family finally became convinced, and in October 1928 three families totaling fifteen people made their departure from Russia. They came first to a beautiful, fertile land called Latvia, and everyone but Mama wanted to stay there. But Mama listened to the Spirit and was firm in insisting that they leave Asia completely. They traveled a long distance on land before reaching the ship that would take them to Mexico. My

172

family later learned that many of the Latvian people had been killed by the Communists. They also found that they had been among the last group of people to legally leave Russia.

As their ship docked at the port of Veracruz, Mexico, they found that entrance to the United States was rarely permitted during that period of near-depression. While waiting the next 3½ years, the families' desire to come to the United States increased. They set out on their journey to the border with their car so overloaded with belongings that it was necessary to tie their spare tires on the sides of the automobile. Some rode, but most walked almost the entire distance along the primitive road through the wilderness and thick jungle. Many times they had no water. Yet this was a time of singing and prayer because my father, who was their leader, would be guided by the Spirit to find water. They could then continue their journey refreshed and renewed.

When they reached Ensenada, they went often to the Mexican Consul to ask permission to cross to the United States but were always refused. My sister Vera was retarded, and her condition had previously prevented the family from entering the United States. My brothers and sisters were worried, but Mama was inspired by the Spirit to say that the Lord would see that the eyes of the authorities would be blinded to her condition.

Finally the Kalinchenkos received permission to enter because Papa was a minister, and no further mention was made about my sister Vera. My family traveled first to San Francisco because many Russian people had previously settled there and were expecting their minister to arrive.

As they continued to follow the Spirit, opportunities opened up. After living in the Bay Area for a time, the families eventually settled in Los Angeles County, where they quickly attached themselves to a small group of European Christians. Through suffering and persecution these people too had learned what it meant to live for Christ, and they deeply appreciated the freedom to worship. My father, John Kalinchenko, soon became a naturalized citizen and shortened his name to Kaline. During this time Manya and I, the last of the ten Kalinchenko children, were born.

Through the years we struggled and sacrificed to sponsor many families from Russia to the United States. In this way our small congregation of Bethany Baptists grew to include two services, one in English and the other in Russian, where we were taught strict obedience to the commandments of God.

Jacqueline's Story

Shortly after the birth of our third child I came in contact with The Church of Jesus Christ of Latter-day Saints. I had always believed the principles of the gospel but did not know they existed in a formalized religion. Still I disagreed much of the time during my instruction and tried to confuse the missionaries. They were constant and true to their work, however, and had the Holy Ghost to guide them. After listening and praying, I began to know what was true as the Spirit bore witness to me, line upon line and precept upon precept. Within three months I was a member, becoming baptized on June 14, 1961.

Being in the Church without my husband and without the approval of parents and family caused me to face many challenges and experience some doubts; but with help from the Saints, especially from a dear sister who took great interest in my behalf, my testimony grew strong and firm. The Lord blessed me often with sweet experiences and memories that I could never deny.

One night I had a dream in connection with my husband's family. I saw myself speaking to a congregation which seemed to be in midair above the pews of a chapel. I was speaking to them in Russian, bearing my testimony as to the truthfulness of the gospel. The colors in the dream were beautiful, and as I spoke the people seemed very happy.

On the front row the first person I recognized (from a photo) was Bill's mother, who had passed away when he was a boy. She

174

seemed to be saying to them, "Listen, listen!" Mostly peasants were in the next rows, but others were also in ornate dress as if to show me the time and circumstance in which they lived. The dream faded as quickly as it came. I now knew that those Russian people in the spirit world were anxious to be progressing in the gospel path.

I felt impressed that I must prepare their names for the temple. Later I wondered why the dream should come to *me*. Why not Bill rather than me? I concluded that perhaps he was not ready. Maybe he would not have believed or accepted the dream in the same way that I did. I wondered if it would be left up to me to do the genealogical research for my husband's lines. At that time I did not know how long it would be before Bill joined the Church. Having a strong desire to learn Russian, I took a course in that language for one year. Bill's family was delighted that I was making this effort.

As the years passed I seemed to grow spiritually a little more each year. I had a strong desire for my husband to be in the Church, and I asked the Lord why I had to wait. I was surprised by the answer to my prayers: "You are not ready." I then knew I had to grow a few years more before I was prepared for such a rich blessing. Now I can easily see the Lord's wisdom and can understand his mercy and love during our hard times. I have felt that he often suffers *with* us during our trials.

Bill's father died unexpectedly of a heart attack. We went to be with the family at Papa's home. Some time later I was alone in the kitchen when I felt the presence of someone standing behind me. I stood there quietly and tried to absorb and analyze the feeling. It was a very sweet feeling of love, and I knew at that moment that Bill's mother and father were standing together behind me. I had the impression that his mother was pointing to me, saying, "She is our only hope." I was the only one in the family who had the gospel of Jesus Christ and they were relying on me to be a faithful example so that my husband and I could together have them sealed in the temple as an eternal family.

A few days later we attended Papa's Russian funeral, which was a very spiritual occasion. First a group would sing, then friends would eulogize, and then the group would sing again. The strong beliefs of the Russian people seemed to pervade their music. As they were singing, I kept hearing additional voices. As I listened, I thought, "I'm hearing Papa's voice; I'm hearing him sing." (He had a powerful bass voice. In Russia he had been given an opportunity to sing professionally, but he refused because he felt it was not the Lord's will.)

I kept hearing his voice, and I was crying because I heard it so strongly with the other voices. I whispered to Bill what I had heard. He was weeping also, for he too had heard Papa's voice. It was a testimony to us of the nearness of the spirit world.

As time passed, Bill attended church with me and seemed to feel that the doctrines were logical and right, but he still had many questions. As he began to pray for strength to live the Word of Wisdom and overcome other problems, the Lord was generous in his answers. So direct were the answers he received that he had no further problems from that time forth with things that had troubled him for years. Bill was baptized September 28, 1974.

Bill's Conclusion

We are anxiously striving to do what the Lord requires of us, for how else can we repay him for our many blessings? We feel certain my parents were guided to America for many reasons, the most important being the opportunity for their descendants to have membership in the true Church of Jesus Christ. My own responsibility is great, for I must take the gospel to my family here on earth as well as do the work for those who are still patiently waiting beyond the veil.

Jackie and I and our children have been sealed eternally in the house of the Lord, and the day is fast approaching when we shall be able to enter the holy temple in behalf of my parents, John and Julia Kalinchenko, who are yet very near to us.

A Catholic Does
LDS Research

Rick L. Podoll

My genealogical story has its beginning in Fond du Lac, Wisconsin, where I was born and raised and began my employment. I am from a long line of staunch Catholics, and I had absolutely no interest in genealogy.

Throughout my working life I have normally been regularly employed, but at the time this story begins I had run into a spell of bad luck, and after two unsuccessful attempts to stay employed I was quite despondent. One morning I asked the Lord to show me what to do and to open the doors of his way in my life. I was in a constant state of prayer in my mind and heart for about two weeks, yet nothing seemed to happen.

One day my brother Danny, who lived in Utah, came to see me. He asked my wife, Ruth Ann, and me to come to Utah. I flatly refused and thought to myself: "There is no way you're getting me to Utah. It's not for me, with all those crazy Mormons living there." But that night my wife prayed and the Lord told her to go to Utah (with or without me). When she told me this the next morning a terrible argument developed, and we did not speak to each other until the day we left.

On that day, she said: "All of your things are packed. You can either come or stay behind, but I'm going to Utah."

177

"But, Honey," I said, "there is probably no Catholic church where you want to go and I don't even have a job there!"

Off we went anyway. It was not until we were in Iowa that I realized we had only $54 to finish the trip. I yelled, "There is no way we can get to Utah with only $54 and a car that uses gas as though it were water!" Then she started to cry and said, "Honey, just trust in God and we'll make it."

On we went through Iowa and Nebraska, but when we got to Laramie, Wyoming, we only had enough money left for one tank of gas. We had over four hundred miles to go and only a little over three hundred miles' worth of gas.

As we pulled into the gas station, Ruth Ann said she would pump the gas. We spent all the money we had on gas. She made the sign of the cross and said, "Lord, help us in doing your commandment." When she hopped in the car she said, "Rick, say a prayer, because we're broke."

On we went. When we got to Evanston, Wyoming, our gas gauge was on empty. Ruth Ann just kept on driving. The gas gauge registered empty from Evanston to Nephi, Utah. When we arrived at my brother's home the car just stopped dead. Ruth got out of the car and said with joy, "Thank you, Lord." I sat back dumbfounded.

On the second Monday in July I was talking to one of our new neighbors in Nephi, Utah. She told me how important family research is in the LDS Church. Being a Roman Catholic and very new to the Mormon way of salvation, I just laughed at what she said to me; but I couldn't forget it and I didn't know why.

A couple of days later, Ruth Ann and I and a friend went to the camping grounds on Mt. Nebo for a picnic. As we were eating, my interest was attracted to a family who arrived in a red van. An older woman and her family sat down at a picnic table not far from us. I got the strangest feeling that I should talk to her about genealogy, but I thought to myself: "Rick, you don't even know her; she's going to think you are out of your mind. Why do you want to know about genealogy anyway?"

Just as we were almost ready to go I was so overwhelmed by this feeling that I was drawn up out of my seat, and before I knew it I was standing in front of her introducing myself. I asked her if she knew anything about genealogy. When she said that she had been doing research work for over twenty-five years, I almost fell over. As the conversation proceeded, she invited me to her home to discuss genealogy further. Her name was Lorraine Hayes and she owned the Nephi Floral. By this time my wife and Gail, our friend, were ready to leave, so I said goodbye and we left.

A couple of days later I went over to Lorraine's home. She told me why she did genealogical research, and I sort of laughed at her on the inside. I told her that the only reason I wanted to look up my past relatives was that I was curious as to who they were and where they came from.

For a second she was silent. Then she looked me straight in the face and said, "Rick, you were brought out to Utah for a great mission in the Lord's work for the dead." I was spellbound for a minute at what she said to me. I thought to myself: "Lady, you are crazy. You don't know me from Adam. How can you sit there and say such a thing?" Then I brushed it off by thinking, "Oh, those crazy Mormons and their beliefs!" After a while she asked me to meet some of her friends, and then I decided to go home.

That night, while sitting home with Ruth Ann, I started to think about temple sealing and work for the dead. As Ruth Ann and I talked about it she said we could still go to the LDS Genealogical Library in Salt Lake and do research work, even if we didn't believe in the Mormon religion. So we made arrangements to go to the library the following Friday.

At the library I could not find a thing. After dinner I decided to give up, but as I was about to leave, a lady came up to me and said, "The information you want is right over here." I followed her to a drawer containing 1870 censuses. She handed me one from Waushara County, Wisconsin. As I turned around to thank her she was gone. It puzzled me, but I soon forgot about it.

I put the film on the reader, and with the first few turns of the handle I found the names of my great-grandparents. The census told me that my relatives, Johann and Caroline Podoll, came from Prussia. I went up and looked in the Prussian records on the European floor in the library, but when I got up there I started helping other people by translating German script. (My father and Grandmother Scott on my mother's side started to teach me German when I was very small.) I spent the rest of the day helping others, and when the library closed I went home almost empty-handed.

On our way home I started thinking about the lady who had helped me find the census record. It struck me that I had seen her before somewhere, but I could not place her. That night at home as I was paging through one of our photograph books, I saw her picture. She was Augusta Bliskey Podoll, my dad's mother; but she died five years before I was born. I wondered why tears came to my eyes. I thought: "What's happening to me? First there was the way I met Lorraine, and then I saw my dead grandmother. Am I losing my mind? Dead people don't come back, because once you are dead you're dead. It is just impossible." And I thought further, "I am really sick."

When my wife came home from my brother's house, I didn't say anything about my experience. (You just don't go around telling people that you have seen a dead person, and I didn't know how she would take it.) Later on that night I saw my grandmother again and felt her very close to me. I didn't sleep the rest of the night. I promised myself I would never tell anyone what happened; I was so afraid of what people would think.

A couple of days later I was talking to a lady named Delis Painter of Nephi. Suddenly she started to tell me how her mother had come back from the dead and how she had guided her and her daughter home from a long trip on a foggy night. As she told me this I froze inside and thought that maybe the dead really *do* come back. Reluctantly I told her what had happened to me, and she believed me. I was not going crazy! She believed! I felt as though I were on top of the world that night.

One day a couple of weeks later Lorraine said to me, "The Lord has a mission for you, Rick," but I still didn't think too much about it.

After some time Ruth Ann and I went back to the library in Salt Lake City. I went to the area where I could look over the Prussian records, but again I ended up helping other people. I found that as a result of helping others with their research problems I would be led to find something important on my own lines. Just before closing time I got a very strange feeling to find a certain book. In my mind I could see the book I wanted, but in reality I had never seen it.

I let my feet guide me. When I walked by the Wisconsin aisle I saw the book at the end of the aisle. It seemed as though it was the only book on the whole shelf. I picked up the book and it flopped open to a story about my great-grandfather's brother on my mother's side, L. D. Scott; and it told me that the Scotts came from Pennsylvania. With that information I went home.

A week later I returned to the library with Lorraine. When I walked in I started to pick out books on Pennsylvania. Within one hour I had found records of my people from Pennsylvania and all the other families that were related through surnames. Those records took me to New Hampshire, Connecticut, and Massachusetts. Within six glorious hours at the library I accomplished work on the Seeleys from 1878 in Pennsylvania to 1537 in England, and on the Scotts from 1965 in Wisconsin to 1730 in Roxbury, Massachusetts.

The Spirit was really with me. What the Spirit was I did not know; but I knew that I was guided by someone. That day I found the marriage dates, birth dates, and death records for over 375 people. When I got home I had a lot of work to do, but within a week I had my pedigree charts and family group sheets completed.

Then a very strange thing happened. About seven o'clock one evening a lady from the spirit world stood before me and said: "I am the grandmother you cannot find. My name is Darcy Hamilton, by Massachusetts, via Connecticut." She was dressed in the most beautiful white clothing I have ever seen. Her face and hands radiated with a transformed glow. I have never seen anything so glorious in my life.

She extended her arms and said to me, "You are the key to our salvation." As she said this, four men appeared on her left. The men were my Scott ancestors — my grandfathers Jesse (who died in 1965), his father Levi (who died in 1905), his father Luke (who died in 1836), and *his* father Luke (who died about 1806). They were wearing street clothes of their era, and none of them looked happy or at peace with himself. My grandfather Jesse Marion Scott had the face of a young man, yet somehow at the same time he was old. I can remember going to his funeral and how upset I felt. As a little boy I had asked myself why my grandpa had to die and leave us all here alone. When I saw him standing there, all those memories came back.

Three women also appeared on the right of my grandmother, and they also were my grandparents from the Scott side. They too were dressed in street clothes of their day. As they stood in front of me, my grandmother in white said, "Ricky, the spirits of the living, the dead, the past, and the future have brought you to Utah that you might help them." Then she said, "What is bound on earth, let it be bound in heaven; and what is bound in heaven, let it also be bound on earth." After she said this she brought her hands together and the men and women vanished. Her last words to me were: "My son, remember, just remember what I have said to you. You are the key to our salvation." With those words she disappeared.

When she had gone I just stood there, wondering what had

182

happened to me. I had to pinch myself to see if I was awake or if I had dreamed it all. I was bewildered about everything.

After a while, when I had composed myself, I went to a family home evening to which Lorraine Hayes and my wife and I were invited. When I saw Lorraine I told her everything that had happened to me earlier. When I finished she was crying. She asked me to describe to her the apparel of the lady dressed in white. She explained to me that it was the clothing worn in the holy temples. With that we both wept, and we agreed that the thing to do was to send their names to the temple.

In rechecking the archive records, I found my grandmother Darcy Hamilton listed as Mary Trott. She was the only one of my ancestors who appeared on an archive sheet as having her temple ordinance work done. She was the same person as the Darcy Hamilton who had appeared to me dressed in temple clothing and who had radiated such a beautiful spirit. These facts I discerned as I discovered her records:

Mary Trott, forbidden by her father John Trott to marry her cousin, John Scott, took upon herself the name of her beloved cousin Darcy Hamilton (who had died at age three).

John Scott and Darcy Hamilton (Mary Trott) lived in Massachusetts, married in Connecticut, and later moved to New Hampshire to avoid persecution. Though the records were hazy in many respects, the will of John Scott cleared up the mystery and confirmed that Darcy Hamilton was in reality Mary Trott Scott.

When I found her name in the archives, bubbles of happiness welled up within me. She was *my* grandmother! She was listed with her parents and family and had not been sealed to her husband, John Scott. At time of writing, that work is in process of being done.

When she appeared to me stating her name, I was then able to connect her to the Scott family through the marriage record and other research which proved her true identity.

Later my wife and I went to Lorraine's house and filled out over fifty entry sheets with my ancestors' names. When we went to the library a couple of days later we handed in the sheets.

My experiences in genealogy have proven to me that our people are waiting patiently on the other side and are counting on us. If there is one thing more that I have learned, it is that the Lord works in many wonderful ways and that if we will just make the effort he will see us through to the end.

(Compilers' note: Ricky and Ruth Ann Podoll were baptized into the Church while this book was being produced — February 26, 1977.)